MAGICAL THOUGHT
IN CREATIVE WRITING

BY THE SAME AUTHOR
Traditional Romance and Tale:
How Stories Mean
(D. S. Brewer Ltd)

ANNE WILSON

Magical Thought in Creative Writing

*The Distinctive Roles
of Fantasy and Imagination
in Fiction*

THE THIMBLE PRESS

To the memory of my cousin
Ruth Clive Ellis
of Stratford-upon-Avon

British Library Cataloguing in
Publication Data
Wilson, Anne
Magical thought in creative writing
1. Fiction – History and criticism
I. Title
809.3   PN3451

ISBN 0-903355-09-4

© Anne Wilson 1983
Printed in Great Britain for
The Thimble Press
Station Road, South Woodchester,
Stroud, Glos. GL5 5EQ
by Short Run Press Ltd., Exeter
Phototypeset in 10/11½ pt Linoterm Baskerville
by Paragon Photoset, Aylesbury
First published 1983

CONTENTS

Preface, 7

Introduction, 15

1. *She*, 37
2. *Jane Eyre*, 48
3. Two Stories by H. C. Andersen, 62
    I. *The Ugly Duckling*, 62
    II. *The Shadow*, 66
4. *The Lord of the Rings*, 70
5. *The Wife of Bath's Tale*, 82
6. *Sir Gawain and the Green Knight*, 94
    I. *Sir Gawain and the Green Knight* and *The Grene Knight*, 94
    II. *Sir Gawain and the Green Knight* and *The Lord of the Rings*, 107
7. *Hamlet*, 114
    I. Shakespeare's Play, 115
    II. The Source Material and the Play, 125

Towards a Conclusion, 140

Notes, 145

Index, 155

ACKNOWLEDGEMENTS

The author's thanks are due to the proprietors of the copyrights in the following works quoted in the text: *From Cuchulainn to Gawain: Sources and Analogues of 'Sir Gawain and the Green Knight'*, by Elisabeth Brewer (D. S. Brewer, Ltd); *The Complete Grimm's Fairy Tales*, by Jakob Ludwig Karl Grimm and Wilhelm Karl Grimm, translated by Margaret Hunt and James Stern (Copyright 1944 by Pantheon Books, Inc., and renewed 1972 by Random House, Inc.; reprinted by permission of Pantheon Books, a Division of Random House, Inc.).

PREFACE

Many may wonder what the excuse is for yet one more book on the nature of storytelling. The amount of work done on the theory of fiction is already formidable, these labours beginning with those of Aristotle, and enormously added to this century by the work of the structuralists and a variety of other scholars. However, scholars, perhaps because of their occupational partiality for reasoning and, in the case of literary scholars, for imaginative art, have paid scant attention to the role played by primitive, magical thought (fantasy) in the creation of fictional literature.

I first became aware of this omission some years ago, when I was making a study of the medieval romances and other traditional literature (which was published in *Traditional Romance and Tale*[1]). Since many of these stories are created by magical thought, the absence of any study of it amazed me. When preparing this present book on fiction of individual authorship (as opposed to traditional literature), I found that magical thought plays a smaller part here, while nevertheless a significant one. In some of these fictions magical thought has created the plot, and the author's imagination – an entirely distinct level of thought – has then worked upon this magical material. This gave me an opportunity to study the different ways in which magical story creation and the author's imagination may operate together; I was also able to discover more about the behaviour of magical thought as it creates a story.

Primitive fantasy has, of course, been a concern of psychiatric medicine, and the ideas of Freud and Jung have played a role in literary criticism. The two psychiatrists themselves and their successors, from Jones[2] to Bettelheim[3], have applied their knowledge to literature, and there has been some psychological analysis of story material, of characters in fiction, and of writers through their fictions; there has also been study of how writers have used psychoanalysis in their art.[4] None of these studies firmly isolates the magical level of thought from imaginative thought in order to study the magical creative process. Bruno Bettelheim, for example, sees folktales as symbolic expressions of a thought which is able to encompass both fantasy and a rational contemplation of the outer world. Furthermore, while irrational, subliminal material has interested scholars such as Derek Brewer[5] and Stephen Prickett[6], this psychological interest still does not isolate magical creative activity: instead, fragmentary manifestations of fantasy (for example, certain sexual fantasies and 'the family drama') are included in studies which are primarily concerned with imaginative art.

Imaginative art, in contradistinction to magical fictions, is created by thought which looks outward from the self to consider the world at large and which explores the inner self in the light of a contemplation of the external world. These very qualities lead to its operating quite differently from magical thinking. It is this level of thought which Dr Brewer describes, when he explores stories as symbolic representations of maturation, and which Dr Prickett is also concerned with, in exploring how the Victorians evolved unique forms of fantasy. Magical thinking is unable to concern itself with the preparation of the individual for life in the world at large (although it sometimes conjures up a helpful change of feeling), and it is not a method of thought altered by cultural changes. Nowhere has there been a systematic attempt to explore how magical thought – irrational, solipsistic and wielding powers made possible by its unconcern with external realities – has played a role wholly distinct from that of the imagination in the creation of entire fictions.

Magical fantasy cannot be confused with 'ethically controlled fantasy', which is what Robert Scholes means by 'fabulation'.[7] While 'ethically controlled fantasy' is created by writers turning away from the techniques of mimesis (the imitation of perceived reality), I would describe both these fictional techniques as imaginative art. Ethics are obviously a concern of rational levels of thought, and Scholes' 'fabulation' is described as created by reason. We are also told that it is allegorical, its practitioners using allegory because they do not naively believe that they can capture the actual world as do those practising realism.[8] 'Fabulation' is further described as a return to a more verbal and artistic kind of fiction.[9] Allegory, verbal expression and artistry are all concerns of imaginative art.

Tzvetan Todorov, in *The Fantastic*[10], is equally concerned with imaginatively contrived 'fantasy'. He describes the 'themes of the self' as showing characteristics which I also find in fantasy (such as multiplication of the personality and the collapse of the limit between subject and object), but he is not describing the same phenomenon as I am describing. He defines the 'fantastic' as lasting only as long as reader and character hesitate, wondering whether that which they perceive derives from what is commonly regarded as reality. At the story's end the reader makes his decision, thereby emerging from the fantastic: if he decides that the laws of reality remain intact and permit an explanation of the phenomena described, then he has opted for the genre of the 'uncanny'; and if he decides that new laws of nature must be entertained to account for the phenomena, he has opted for the genre of the 'marvellous'. In the case of the fantasy I am concerned with, readers do not do this, for, fantastic and nonsensical as this fantasy appears to our rational minds, readers on the whole never compare its events with what they perceive as external reality.

While magical fantasy exists permanently in the mind, subordinated only part of the time to the directed, more laborious thinking of reason and the imagination, the two levels of thought tend to be strangers to each other, the enjoyment of fantasy taking place without there being any surprise or even interest on the part of the 'higher' levels of thought. Audiences will enjoy a fantasy and perhaps laugh at it afterwards, but they will not find it puzzling unless they are asked to explain it; it does not normally occur to anyone to ask for an explanation in depth and, far from seeming confused, audiences clearly find it deeply meaningful. In other words, the nonsense of fantasy only appears as nonsense to part of our minds, and that part (the rational part) does not become engaged during the enjoyment of a fantasy. Another difference between Todorov's study and my own is that he illustrates some of his 'themes of the self' from Gautier's experiences under the influence of hashish, while the fantasy I describe is normal, everyday experience, whether we are aware of it or not. Todorov, moreover, does not distinguish clearly between fantasy contrived by imaginative ingenuity and the spontaneous, naïve magical fantasy which I describe, while I contend that magical fantasy can be clearly distinguished, since it creates discernible and characteristic story structures which I have analysed, using some of the methods of Vladimir Propp.[11]

While I use some structuralist techniques, my approach has to be different from that of Propp and his successor Todorov. Propp compares a large number of stories and discerns behind the variety of action and character just a few types of action and character function. For example, he notes that during an adventure the hero may be helped by a magically powerful character to whom he has proved himself worthy of help; this character may be an old woman, a dwarf, a dead man, a prisoner or an animal, but behind these diverse characters is their recurrent function in that they are 'donors', whose help is the result of the hero's passing a test of character. Todorov, who also uses the comparative method, observes[12] that all narrative is a movement between two equilibria which are similar but not identical. At the start of the narrative there is always a stable situation, for example, a child living in the micro-society of his family, with its laws. Then a disequilibrium is brought about, causing the child to leave home. At the end of the story, after overcoming many obstacles, the child returns home, grown up to a re-established equilibrium. A supernatural event may intervene to break the median disequilibrium and provoke the long quest for the second equilibrium: being external to the situation in the narrative and also to the world itself, the supernatural is the best means of disturbing the stable situation of the beginning. Working on *The Decameron* in *Grammaire du Décameron*[13] Todorov extends an inventory of narrative possibilities.

My analysis is not done by comparison: instead, I examine each work of fiction in isolation from other works. I was originally prompted to study works in strict isolation when examining the medieval romances, since my concern was to discover how the seemingly crazy elements of these romances could be preserved faithfully in oral tradition even while they could not be explained rationally; there was something knitting them together. This 'something' was discerned by giving attention to every detail, which the reductionist structuralists do not do, and also by giving attention to the narrative order of the story's transmission to us, which Claude Lévi-Strauss does not do.[14] By concentrating on each story on its own terms, as audiences do, and then distancing myself from the story for an objective examination of how it works, I observed a scheme at the heart of it which could be seen to have given rise to its every element. This scheme cannot be seen from the position outside the story which the structuralists have adopted; it can only be seen if one identifies with the hero or heroine of the story and views the events and characters, including the protagonist's presentation of himself, as the protagonist's own creation. The reason for this is that audiences identify with the protagonist and, while they do this to some extent in the case of all stories, in the case of magical fantasy identification must be total, since magical fantasy has no detached author. Even when we view such a fantasy as its hero's own invention, it will not make sense if we assume that the hero is contriving the fantastic events with an awareness of the world external to himself. He will not, as in the case of stories studied by Todorov, decide to introduce the supernatural because it is external to the situation of the story or to the world, for he is engaged in a level of thought which is entirely magical and exclusively concerned with the affairs of his inner world.

In *The Fantastic* Todorov suggests that supernatural beings in a narrative compensate for a deficient causality, a fairy who assures a character's fortunate destiny being no more than the incarnation of an imaginary causality for what might just as well be called chance, while an ill-disposed genie is none other than the hero's bad luck.[15] In the study of the primitive fantasy I describe, there can be no useful appraisal of the material according to rational ideas. The usurping waiting-maid in *The Goose-Girl*, which I discuss in my Introduction, could never be interpreted as the heroine's bad luck, for, in the fantasy structure which I identify, she has the purposeful role of expressing a vision that the heroine has of herself which conflicts with an opposing vision, and it is this conflict which propels the story. It will be noticed that the waiting-maid is hardly a fairy or a genie, but, at the level of thought which I study, a waiting-maid has magical powers, for all the thought creating the story is magical: the thoughts of the protagonist creating the story become deeds and events at once, and the adventure, with its excitement and fear, is created largely by the conflict of these magical thoughts. If the hero introduces a fairy or genie into his fantasy, that character may be invested with particular magical powers, these magical powers often made tangible or otherwise fixed in magic objects or words, which can give the hero a feeling that he has greater control over the thoughts and wishes in the story.

Those to whom this level of thinking is unstudied terrain may feel inclined to dismiss it or may wonder how any systematic study can be made of the fictions it creates. It was the purpose of my book *Traditional Romance and Tale* to explore how it could be done in the case of traditional literature, and it is one of the purposes of this book to explore how it may be done in relation to fictions created by individual authors. As the study of *The Goose-Girl* in my Introduction shows, the study of fantasy in a folktale is a simpler task than the study of fantasy in a novel, for in a folktale magical thought may be the only creative activity and the morphology of the fiction which it creates is comparatively clear. In the case of the work of individual authors, wherever there may be a magical fantasy present, there may also have been creative activity on the part of the imagination, and this makes the task more complicated. I contend that only a complete fantasy is capable of being reliably tested by systematic study, and I shall therefore not be concerned with fragments of fantasy. Moreover, in the interests of systematic analysis, I devote this book to a few detailed studies rather than to many, briefer studies.

It may be objected that such a primitive level of thought can hardly have been involved in the creation of our greatest literature, but, while the activity of the imagination has been paramount in the creation of these works, a fantasy may also have been used. For instance, a study of Chaucer's *The Wife of Bath's Tale* can be enriched by a grasp of the traditional fantasy which Chaucer uses and transforms for his imaginative purposes. Furthermore, I believe that the study of some literary works has been unsatisfactory because of an apparent unawareness that magical thought has played a major role in their creation. *Hamlet* is a notable example: while there has been much Freudian study of the play, no one has traced the magical fantasy structure to be found in the versions of the Hamlet story given by Saxo Grammaticus and Belleforest, which are Shakespeare's likely sources. Shakespeare has re-created and modified this fantasy in a most interesting way, and also transformed parts of it with his imaginative art. Similarly, in the case of *Jane Eyre*, a critic has written, 'Jane Eyre. . . . and St. John Rivers submit briefly to the power of fantasy but are not overwhelmed by it'[16]: the curious features of the novel, and its odd coincidences and repetitions, which make no sense either at the level of realism or at the level of 'ethically controlled fantasy', are not explored. As these works often puzzle students, I am surprised that the questions they raise, such as 'Why isn't Hamlet king?' (not really answered by the Danish laws of succession, since the audience was Elizabethan) have been paid so little attention.

The study of magical thought in fiction is a difficult task. The irrational has a habit of being inscrutable under the gaze of reason, and, since fantasy is subjective material, which may be absorbed by audiences without the examination to which they might submit imaginative material, it can be elusive. It is also apt to mean many things at once. Consequently, interpretation must always be insufficient and uncertain, and it is unfortunate that I have to give interpretations – with some confidence – in order to produce coherent explanations of what I see happening in a story. My aim is not to know what stories mean so much as to explore, through a few detailed studies, what magical storytelling is, how it contrasts with the creativity of the imagination – in particular, imaginatively contrived fantasy – and how it may appear in the work of individual authors as opposed to traditional romance and folktale.

A combination of circumstances has given me the experience of discovering a new approach to an important area of fiction. I came to work on the medieval romances – pursuing a quite different matter for a Ph.D. – after a decade in Africa and after an experience of psychoanalysis. In Africa I had been engaged in language research (I specialized in language for my first degree in English at Manchester University), but I also became interested in the role of magic in society there; under psychoanalysis, moreover, I learnt how to observe magical thinking in myself. At the same time, I was able to observe my own children's experiences with stories and dreams. It was also a help, as a teacher and researcher, not to be heavily committed to the verbal level of thought: I was the more free to look critically at the central position we give to the verbal level, when I came to teach at a further education college and consider how few of us use it with skill. Finally, my career did not depend on my satisfying examiners for a doctorate, so I was able to take the risk of making magical fantasy my area of research. In these circumstances, I was faced with a great body of stories which seemed quite crazy but must have meaning. I was able to resist the temptation to mistreat them as symbolic expressions of well-known notions in the world at large, because I wished to pursue the nonsense and was quite prepared to find that the stories had an unexpected, internal logic. Thus I stumbled on the subject which I have now explored for ten years. It has taken me many years to come to my present understanding of magical stories, but in the early stages the notion that identification was the key – that magical stories had to be viewed as the creation of the hero – opened up a fascinating new area of fictional creation with much more to be discovered.

I began my research for this present book before my first book was published (it spent many years looking for a publisher), and since my subject matter was now the complex fiction of individual authors, I was able to learn much more about magical creative activity and its operation in relation to imaginative art. My first study was *Hamlet*, made in 1975–6, and I believe that this research has done much to elucidate the famous problems in the play. All told, I have studied hundreds of stories, both magical and imaginative, but for this book I have chosen just those which I think will explain my findings best. I am aware of the difficulty involved in following some of my discussion – magical thinking is sometimes extremely complicated – and I have therefore arranged my chapters so that readers can get all my main points from the first half of the book, if they so wish, without having to tackle the more strenuous second half. The earlier chapters develop the argument and the last three show how it can be applied to more complex works.

I have not included a bibliography since very few publications have directly assisted my research. My notes, however, include full details of both relevant and contrasting studies.

In the preparation of this book, I am particularly indebted to my husband, Anthony Wilson, and to Professor Geoffrey T. Shepherd of Birmingham University, Professor Dorothy Emmet and Mr Lawrence King, who read the manuscript and made many valuable criticisms and suggestions. My gratitude goes, too, to Dr David Blamires of Manchester University, Mrs Wendy Robinson, lay analyst, Dr Sigvard von Sicard of the Selly Oak Colleges, Birmingham, Dr Graham Hope Scott, and to the late Professor Roy Pascal for their help and advice; and also to Professors Joseph P. Haughton and Gordon Quinn of Trinity College, Dublin, for their help when I was seeking access to all the Irish versions of the Loathly Lady story. As this book has had even more difficulty than the last in finding a publisher, I am particularly grateful to those who have assisted and encouraged me during the three and a half years of searching. Above all, I am grateful to Nancy and Aidan Chambers, of *Signal* magazine and The Thimble Press, for publishing the book. I would also like to remember the help of Mr Kenneth A. Cory, Librarian at Western Montana College, Professor Neville G. Brown of Birmingham University, Mr Anthony Sheil of Anthony Sheil Associates, Ltd. and Mrs Elaine Turner of Schiller College, in Kent. Finally, my gratitude goes to Mrs Joyce Miller, who worked in a most helpful partnership with me, typing out my first manuscript and also the revisions I made in 1980.

ANNE D. WILSON
Birmingham, April 1982

INTRODUCTION

Having given my excuses for writing this book in the Preface, I shall devote this Introduction to defining what I mean by fantasy and to tracing how it is distinct from the activity of the imagination. I shall begin with definitions and then illustrate my definition of fantasy through a discussion of *The Goose-Girl*, a folktale, which will be given in full. Briefer discussions of *The Emperor's New Clothes* and *Treasure Island* will help to show how imaginative art operates differently in the creation of a story.

Fantasy is a form of thinking which is magical in character, 'magical' because it is free from the laws and realities of the external world, and therefore operates with special powers to bring things about. These things are brought about in the mind alone, of course, but that is its realm: it is focused exclusively on the affairs of the inner world of the mind, taking no heed of those outside. Since magical thought is not concerned with outer reality, it does not engage in searching reflection; it does not reason, calculate, work out strategies or exercise discriminating judgement. We must all be aware, at times, of its activity in our everyday lives. For example, there are times when we may consider another person, or the world, wholly in the light of our own feelings or wishes, thus 'making them up' rather than examining evidence or engaging in an imaginative effort to see points of view other than our own. We may also be aware, sometimes, of our use of magical rituals and talismans to give power to our wishes. These things we may discount as mere lapses from intelligent thinking, but they are manifestations of another, important, level of thinking which takes distinctive forms, particularly in the fictions it creates. While magical thought may sometimes resort to magic words, the language in which it expresses itself is not primarily verbal: it is primarily pictorial – as is apparent in dreams, which are creations of magical thought – and, thus, the structure which it creates as it tells a story is fundamentally a sequence of images. Words are used to communicate a magical fiction to others, but magical thinking does not itself struggle for precision of expression through diction. The creator of a magical fiction is not distanced from his subject matter; far from this, the essential identification of the creator and re-creators of such a fantasy with the chief character in it suggests that the fantasy should be viewed as the magical creation of this chief character. Since audiences follow a fantasy by identifying with its hero or heroine, and thinking magically, those investigating such a story should also, as part of their study, engage in the story in this fashion.

The imagination also 'makes' the world 'up', of course: our perceptions must always be governed and limited by conditions within the mind. But it does so in ways quite different from those of magical thought. Far from being a spontaneous response to fear, desires and other feelings, shaping the world according to their dictates and resorting to abracadabra methods, the imagination labours to understand the outer world beyond the solipsistic concerns of the inner world, and to deal with it effectively. It makes the effort to recognize the 'otherness' of people and the world, and to grasp other points of view, using the evidence of the senses and dispassionate observation and thought. It is also able to contemplate the inner world, doing this in the light of its observation of the outer one; it is thus able to include magical thinking in its contemplation of reality, and to 'place' and govern it. The imagination is, furthermore, a creative power of the mind which can leap to fresh concepts and unique visions of life, while fantasy is confined to the familiar, since it is concerned only with the expression of the unchanging common stock of human feelings. The imagination can conceive of situations and explore circumstances beyond the owner's experience and which may never have existed. It also labours to unify our experience of the world, through its power to make forms out of the formless. Coleridge, in Chapter Thirteen of his *Biographia Literaria*, describes the imagination as having to do with perception and the conscious will, and as being a power which 'dissolves, diffuses, dissipates, in order to re-create'.

In fictions created by the imagination, the author is distanced from his material, which means that his attitude to it is an important feature of his art: in a fantasy, we are concerned with the hero's mood, while, in imaginative art, we are concerned with the author's tone. An imaginative fiction gives a variety of points of view, as a result of the development of a variety of characters, with their individual personalities, motivation and circumstances; in a magical fiction, there is only the protagonist's point of view, and all the characters are the creation of his own feelings. While the author of an imaginative fiction may or may not be concerned with realism, he will be concerned with creating a world in which we use the methods of thought we apply to affairs in the external world. As the creation takes place predominantly at the verbal level, diction is an important feature, and metaphor and symbolism, which are quite distinct from the dreamlike images and symbols of fantasy, may be employed.

The folktale of *The Goose-Girl*[1], as collected by the Brothers Grimm, will now be given in full.

The Goose-Girl

There was once upon a time an old Queen whose husband had been dead for many years, and she had a beautiful daughter. When the princess grew up she was betrothed to a prince who lived at a great distance. When the time came for her to be married, and she had to journey forth into the distant kingdom, the aged Queen packed up for her many costly vessels of silver and gold, and trinkets also of gold and silver; and cups and jewels, in short, everything which appertained to a royal dowry, for she loved her child with all her heart. She likewise sent her maid-in-waiting, who was to ride with her, and hand her over to the bridegroom, and each had a horse for the journey, but the horse of the King's daughter was called Falada, and could speak. So when the hour of parting had come, the aged mother went into her bedroom, took a small knife and cut her finger with it until it bled. Then she held a white handkerchief to it into which she let three drops of blood fall, gave it to her daughter and said: 'Dear child, preserve this carefully, it will be of service to you on your way.'

So they took a sorrowful leave of each other; the princess put the piece of cloth in her bosom, mounted her horse, and then went away to her bridegroom. After she had ridden for a while she felt a burning thirst, and said to her waiting-maid: "Dismount, and take my cup which you have brought with you for me, and get me some water from the stream, for I should like to drink." "If you are thirsty," said the waiting-maid, "get off your horse yourself, and lie down and drink out of the water, I don't choose to be your servant." So in her great thirst the princess alighted, bent down over the water in the stream and drank, and was not allowed to drink out of the golden cup. Then she said: "Ah, Heaven!" and the three drops of blood answered: "If this your mother knew, her heart would break in two." But the King's daughter was humble, said nothing, and mounted her horse again. She rode some miles further, but the day was warm, the sun scorched her, and she was thirsty once more, and when they came to a stream of water, she again cried to her waiting-maid: "Dismount, and give me some water in my golden cup," for she had long ago forgotten the girl's ill words. But the waiting-maid said still more haughtily: "If you wish to drink, get it yourself, I don't choose to be your maid." Then in her great thirst the King's daughter alighted, bent over the flowing stream, wept and said: "Ah, Heaven!" and the drops of blood again replied: "If this your mother knew, her heart would break in two." And as she was thus drinking and leaning right over the stream, the handkerchief with the three drops of blood fell out of her bosom, and floated away with the water without her observing it, so great was her trouble. The waiting-maid, however, had seen it, and she rejoiced to think that she had now power over the bride, for since the princess had lost the drops of blood, she had become weak and powerless. So now when she wanted to mount her horse again, the one that was called Falada, the waiting-maid said: "Falada is more suitable for me, and my nag will do for you," and the princess had to be content with that. Then the waiting-maid, with many hard words, bade the princess exchange her royal apparel for her own shabby clothes; and at length she was compelled to swear by the clear sky above her, that she would not say one word of this to anyone at the royal court, and if she had not taken this oath she would have been killed on the spot. But Falada saw all this, and observed it well.

    The waiting-maid now mounted Falada, and the true bride the bad horse, and thus they travelled onwards, until at length they entered the royal palace. There were great rejoicings over her arrival, and the prince sprang forward to meet her, lifted the waiting-maid from her horse, and thought she was his consort. She was conducted upstairs, but the real princess was left standing below. Then the old King looked out of the window and saw her standing in the courtyard, and noticed how dainty and delicate and beautiful she was, and instantly went to the royal apartment, and asked the bride about the girl she had with her who was standing down below in the courtyard, and who she was. "I picked her up on my way for a companion; give the girl something to work at, that she may not stand idle." But the old King had no work for her, and knew of none, so he said: "I have a little boy who tends the geese, she may help him." The boy was called Conrad, and the true bride had to help him to tend the geese. Soon afterwards the false bride said to the young King: "Dearest husband, I beg you to do me a favour." He answered: "I will do so most willingly." "Then send for the knacker, and have the head of the horse on which I rode here cut off, for it vexed me on the way." In reality, she was afraid that the horse might tell how she had behaved to the King's daughter. Then she succeeded in making the King promise that it should be done, and the faithful Falada was to die; this came to the ears of the real princess, and she secretly promised to pay the knacker a piece of gold if he would perform a small service for her. There was a great dark-looking gateway in the town, through which morning and evening she had to pass with the geese: would he be so good as to nail up Falada's head on it, so that she might see him again, more than once. The knacker's man promised to do that, and cut off the head, and nailed it fast beneath the dark gateway.

    Early in the morning, when she and Conrad drove out their flock beneath this gateway, she said in passing:

> "Alas, Falada, hanging there!"

Then the head answered:

> "Alas, young Queen, how ill you fare!
> If this your mother knew,
> Her heart would break in two."

Then they went still further out of the town, and drove their geese into the country. And when they had come to the meadow, she sat down and unbound her hair which was like pure gold, and Conrad saw it and delighted in its brightness, and wanted to pluck out a few hairs. Then she said:

> "Blow, blow thou gentle wind, I say,
> Blow Conrad's little hat away,
> And make him chase it here and there,
> Until I have braided all my hair,
> And bound it up again."

And there came such a violent wind that it blew Conrad's hat far away across country, and he was forced to run after it. When he came back she had finished combing her hair and was putting it up again, and he could not get any of it. Then Conrad was angry, and would not speak to her, and thus they watched the geese until the evening, and then they went home.

Next day when they were driving the geese out through the dark gateway, the maiden said:

> "Alas, Falada, hanging there!"

Falada answered:

> "Alas, young Queen how ill you fare!
> If this your mother knew,
> Her heart would break in two."

And she sat down again in the field and began to comb out her hair, and Conrad ran and tried to clutch it, so she said in haste:

> "Blow, blow, thou gentle wind, I say,
> Blow Conrad's little hat away,
> And make him chase it here and there,
> Until I have braided all my hair,
> And bound it up again."

Then the wind blew, and blew his little hat off his head and far away, and Conrad was forced to run after it, and when he came back, her hair had been put up a long time, and he could get none of it, and so they looked after their geese till evening came.

But in the evening after they had got home, Conrad went to the old King, and said: "I won't tend the geese with that girl any longer!" "Why not?" inquired the aged King. "Oh, because she vexes me the whole day long." Then the aged King commanded him to relate what it was that she did to him. And Conrad said: "In the morning when we pass beneath the dark gateway with the flock, there is a horse's head on the wall, and she says to it:

> "Alas, Falada, hanging there!"

And the head replies:

> 'Alas, young Queen how ill you fare!
> If this your mother knew,
> Her heart would break in two.' "

And Conrad went on to relate what happened on the goose pasture, and how when there he had to chase his hat.

The aged King commanded him to drive his flock out again next day, and as soon as morning came, he placed himself behind the dark gateway, and heard how the maiden spoke to the head of Falada, and then he too went into the country, and hid himself in the thicket in the meadow. There he soon saw with his own eyes the goose-girl and the goose-boy bringing their flock, and how after a while she sat down and unplaited her hair, which shone with radiance. And soon she said:

> "Blow, blow, thou gentle wind, I say,
> Blow Conrad's little hat away,
> And make him chase it here and there,
> Until I have braided all my hair,
> And bound it up again."

Then came a blast of wind and carried off Conrad's hat so that he had to run far away, while the maiden quietly went on combing and plaiting her hair, all of which the King observed. Then, quite unseen, he went away, and when the goose-girl came home in the evening, he called her aside, and asked why she did all these things. "I may not tell that, and I dare not lament my sorrows to any human being, for I have sworn not to do so by the heaven which is above me; if I had not done that, I should have lost my life." He urged her and left her no peace, but he could draw nothing from her. Then said he: "If you will not tell me anything, tell your sorrows to the iron-stove there," and he went away. Then she crept into the iron-stove, and began to weep and lament, and emptied her whole heart, and said: "Here am I deserted by the whole world, and yet I am a King's daughter, and a false waiting-maid has by force brought me to such a pass that I have been compelled to put off my royal apparel, and she has taken my place with my bridegroom, and I have to perform menial service as a goose-girl. If this my mother knew, her heart would break in two."

The aged King, however, was standing outside by the pipe of the stove, and was listening to what she said, and heard it. Then he came back again, and bade her come out of the stove. And royal garments were placed on her, and it was marvellous how beautiful she was! The aged King summoned his son, and revealed to him that he had got the false bride who was only a waiting-maid, but that the true one was standing there, as the former goose-girl. The young King rejoiced with all his heart when he saw her beauty and youth, and a great feast was made ready to which all the people and all good friends were invited. At the head of the table sat the bridegroom with the King's daughter at one side of him, and the waiting-maid on the other, but the waiting-maid was blinded, and did not recognise the princess in her dazzling array. When they had eaten and drunk, and were merry, the aged King asked the waiting-maid as a riddle, what punishment a person deserved who had behaved in such and such a way to her master, and at the same time related the whole story, and asked what sentence such a person merited. Then the false bride said: "She deserves no better fate than to be stripped entirely naked, and put in a barrel which is studded inside with pointed nails, and two white horses should be harnessed to it, which will drag her along through one street after another, till she is dead," "It is you," said the aged King, "and you have pronounced your own sentence, and thus shall it be done unto you." And when the sentence had been carried out, the young King married his true bride, and both of them reigned over their kingdom in peace and happiness.

If we compare this story with Hans Christian Andersen's well-known *The Emperor's New Clothes*[2], we can see that both stories contain fantastic features, outstanding among them being the horse's severed head which speaks and the emperor's walking naked in the procession, believing he is wearing garments which could only be seen by those wise and fit for the office they hold. Most of the less startling events also seem unlikely on the face of it. The waiting-maid and the princess appear to be riding alone, since there is no mention of an entourage, which must have intervened to prevent the exchange; and yet there must, logically, have been an entourage to convey the royal dowry mentioned at the beginning of the tale, and audiences know even today that princesses do not travel into a foreign kingdom with only the protection and pomp provided by a single waiting-maid. Meanwhile, the trick played by the rogues in H. C. Andersen's story is also highly unlikely. But audiences would respond that these objections are irrelevant, making the claim for art that it does not represent reality as we usually perceive it; for art presents us with something that is like life but markedly different from it in order to express and define aspects of it. The 'difference' is part of the point: the familiar is made to seem strange, so that we see it again.[3]

When reading *The Emperor's New Clothes* we are put on our mettle, for we quickly recognize that the story is both satirical and metaphoric. We see that it has two levels of meaning, because the literal meaning seems quite impossible among people with five senses in good working order: it creates a world in which people are not made certain of the presence or absence of material and clothing by the sight, touch, sound and smell of them, and yet the story is related with a psychological accuracy which convinces us that it is expressing a view of the human scene. The contrast between the characters' apparent lack of senses and our own experience of the senses jolts us into seeing the author's comic vision of humanity, in which people choose to ignore the evidence of their own perceptions in order to remain high in the estimation of other people. In this way we pass over the literal meaning, much as we enjoy its absurdities, to grasp the second meaning we have been made aware of. The story is a continuous metaphor, chosen by the author to express the more precisely and impressively a vision of the world at large and the comedy he sees in it. It appeals entirely to our reason and to our accurate observation of human behaviour: even as we recognize the unquestioning acceptance of the standard by which men should be judged and the extent to which they will dissemble to avoid being condemned by it, we also engage in making inferences; we seek to deduce precisely and completely what Andersen is portraying in the extended metaphor of everybody saying how marvellous something is while there is nothing there.

It is not to be expected that we would find this kind of controlled wit and power in a folktale. I have chosen a folktale with which to compare Andersen's story because it will illustrate most clearly and briefly the peculiar features of magical fantasy, entirely distinct in kind from Andersen's art. One point which might immediately be made is that we do not sense the presence of a detached narrator manipulating our response through his own skilled management of his arts, such as diction, metaphor and tone; if the lack of a detached narrator is to be expected of a folktale, it must nevertheless be noted, for it is an important feature of all magical fantasy.

It is apparent that we do not grasp the meaning of this story through inference and the bringing to bear of our own knowledge of the world in the process of enjoying the story. The characters and dialogue help to further the narrative, without there being any psychological development or even attempt at realism: the heroine is good and beautiful, the waiting-maid a cruel usurper, the queen a loving mother and the old king fair-minded, while the dialogue has a ritual character. Therefore, any reflection on the world at large might be judged to be expressed entirely through symbolism, but, since such symbols, if there are any, would be rather too obscure to ensure the story's survival in oral and popular tradition, it is difficult to feel convinced that this solves our problem. Meanwhile, we could decide that the story is only light, playful fancy, but those following it at that level might object that the princess, who evidently has money, should buy Falada's life rather than only his head to be nailed beneath the gateway; they might also object to the apparent spinelessness of the princess, a challenging and resourceful heroine being more fun. Some of the features of the story, particularly the severed horse's head and the drops of blood, and its highly formal structure, lead one to feel that, while it does not seem to be concerned with the kind of realities with which *The Emperor's New Clothes* is concerned, it is purposefully giving form to something more than fancy. Moreover, if there were no purpose knitting its elements together, how would they be remembered in oral tradition?

Russell Hoban's discussion of the story[4] sees its content as mythic material originating in ancient harvest rituals, which included animal sacrifice and the stripping of a corn-puppet, sometimes called 'the gander's neck' or 'the bride'. The maid-in-waiting is the season in waiting who strips the harvest bride and replaces her, as the winter replaces the harvest season. During the reign of winter, the true bride (who resembles Persephone) talks to her corn-spirit mother, the head of Falada (Demeter assumes the form of a horse when seeking her daughter). Finally, when her time comes round again, she creeps into the womblike stove to reveal the truth, and this leads to the driving out of winter. Russell Hoban believes that the story's 'word-music' and dreamlike qualities, together with its lack of emotion (particularly when treating the prince's attitude to the destruction of the bride he has taken to bed), support the theory that the tale is not a 'story-story' but a transmission of mythic elements in story form. These mythic elements are products of the collective mind and this is why the content is familiar to all of us: every part of the story expresses our experience, and myth and story keep us in touch with the 'other-than-rational' in us.

This attractive approach tempts us to suspend judgement, but it raises obvious questions. First of all, has the magic used by primitive farmers in their struggle with natural forces really been familiar to all the story's audiences? Moreover, if we are able to appreciate ancient material of this kind, might not its methods of thought be alive today and engaged in creating and re-creating fictions relevant to our present needs? Meanwhile, where is Russell Hoban's evidence for the two girls' representing the harvest and winter seasons? True, winter has inexorable power over summer and it is often unpleasant, but these resemblances are scarcely sufficient to clinch the matter. Furthermore, Demeter's assuming the form of a horse in Greek myth is no reason why Falada should be the old queen (our version of the story calls the horse 'he'). Hoban seems to have sensitively grasped the story's ritual character, and stopped short of following this recognition through.

It is essential to Russell Hoban's explanation that the waiting-maid expresses winter fundamentally for us, as we rehearse the myth. Any gap we see between that girl and the season creates a problem, because it means that we would have to follow the story at two levels, levels which would be too difficult for survival in oral tradition. *The Emperor's New Clothes* is a challenging metaphorical story which could only be preserved in a book, and yet it is less formidable than Hoban's suggestion seems to me. In *The Emperor's New Clothes* the narrative is concerned with the familiar external world, while there are obvious cracks in its realism which point to a larger significance; the larger significance is concerned with a vision of the world also known to us, but not seen as clearly as the story makes us see it. We grasp the story's ultimate significance by concentrating on the details of the narrative. In the case of Hoban's interpretation, unless we can reenact the rite, we are going to have to think metaphorically or symbolically, coping, furthermore, with a puzzling narrative pointing to other significance, which also does not mean anything immediate to us. My response would be that the ritual does mean something immediate to us, and that to discover that meaning we need to resist the temptation to give the story some kind of rational explanation and, instead, face the apparent craziness of the narrative, prepared to find an unexpected internal logic. An investigation into the audience's mental engagement in any story requires submission to the text on its own terms and a dependence on contextual evidence rather than on ideas originating from outside the text concerned; I do not believe that analogues are helpful here.[5]

Psychoanalytical investigation of *The Goose-Girl* also tends to introduce material external to the text, and it does this with less regard for the implications of the story's origin than we find in the folklorist approach. The entirely separate purposes of literary scholars and psychiatrists have prevented their combining their expertise to elucidate the nature of stories. Literary scholars lack a practical, working knowledge of magical thought, while psychiatrists will use a work of literature for medical purposes, without any inquiry into its origin and nature. The unfortunate results of this last are apparent in Bruno Bettelheim's discussion of our story.[6]

Dr Bettelheim sees *The Goose-Girl* as being about the achieving of autonomy. The heroine's leaving home symbolizes her going out into the world, where, at first, she does not wish to give up her dependence, transferring it from her parents to her attendant. She allows the waiting-maid to usurp her golden cup and her place, and this is her undoing. Later in the story, she refuses to allow the goose-boy to usurp strands of her golden hair, and this refusal leads to the dénouement, for the boy is driven to complain about her, this changing her fate. Bettelheim also sees the story as guiding child audiences out of the early Oedipal stage, in which a child feels that her parent of the same sex has usurped her rightful place with the parent of the opposite sex, and taking them to the next, higher, stage, when the child recognizes that it is she who wishes to usurp a position in reality belonging to her parent. *The Goose-Girl*, we are told, warns that one must give up such ideas, because of the terrible retribution which is meted out to those who, for a time, succeed in replacing the rightful marital partner; it is better to accept one's condition as a child. Bettelheim also sees *The Goose-Girl* as containing the important lesson that the parent, even if she is as powerful as a queen, is helpless to assure her child's development to maturity: the child must face the trials of life on her own, the mother's gifts being of no use to her if she does not know how to use them well. We are told that the three drops of blood symbolize sexual maturity and that the stove stands, as does a hearth, for the sanctity and security of home. Surprisingly little is said about Falada's role. Bettelheim is concerned with stories as lessons, suggesting to children in symbolic form how they can deal with life's difficulties and so grow to maturity. He quotes Freud as saying that thought is an exploration of possibilities which avoids all the dangers of actual experimentation, and he tells us that a child's fantasies are his thoughts in such an exploration; he also believes that a child's free associations, where a story is concerned, may be used, as in the case of dream analysis.

The contribution made by Freudians to our understanding of primitive fantasy is unrivalled, but Bettelheim has not used his knowledge appropriately here. It would clearly be ridiculous to accuse him of assigning to oral tradition the psychiatrist's intellectual concern with freeing a child from fantasies and substituting a grasp of reality; he is not concerned with the story's origins but with how it can be used by his profession. Moreover, those who think his approach acceptable may not believe that the story's preservation has depended on a popular comprehension of it. I believe that popular literature must have immediate, practical, popular meaning. If there is fantasy in *The Goose-Girl*, we should not expect to find it surveyed critically by rational thought, since that kind of awareness is not common and it requires an effort beyond any we can assume popular audiences would be prepared to make. We should also not expect rational thought in such a story to be concerned with abstractions.

It is strange that Dr Bettelheim, aware of irrational systems of thought as he must be, does not identify irrational purposes in the story. He finds rational purposes in it, having it the symbolic expression of ideas familiar to his profession and making sense to the rational mind (whether we agree with them or not). He thus uses the same rationalizing and symbolizing techniques generally used by critics. However, he also engages in some useful analysis: an example is where he points out the two parallel attempts to usurp something golden from the heroine and the significance of these in terms of the whole story.

Ease of transmission is an important factor in traditional literature, one sometimes neglected by critics. The conditions of oral transmission favour magical stories and simple imaginative tales rather than the more demanding levels of imaginative thought. The Brer Rabbit tales are a good example of imaginative traditional stories; they are part of the African trickster tradition, concerned with the values of communal life, and both trickery and concern with human relationships are products of rational thought.[7] The biblical parables suggest the level of metaphorical thinking which has been readily appreciated by communities as a whole: they are extended metaphors, but their details are familiar and down-to-earth, and the audience grasps the story's larger meaning by virtue of its absorption in these details; it does not look *through* them to an abstract meaning beyond them.[8] We perhaps should not expect any more abstract content to be grasped beyond the immediate impact of the narrative than we find in those stories. Meanwhile, magical stories may well have predominated in oral tradition, since magical thinking, unchanging through time, is recognized spontaneously and effortlessly by audiences, being, as it is, common property. Awareness of a fantasy being enjoyed is quite unnecessary – in fact, the disguises which fantasy often employs are evidence that audiences enjoy fantasy more if they do not scutinize the source of their enjoyment. Magical thought is only difficult for those seeking to study it.

By contrast with folklore specialists and psychoanalysts, Vladimir Propp would have been concerned with *The Goose-Girl* as a work of art. Using his methods we can observe a structure in which the heroine leaves home, voluntarily as a 'seeker heroine', and engages in an adventure brought about by a villain. The adventure ends with tests in which the unrecognized heroine triumphantly achieves recognition. The recognition is aided by certain marks of proof: the heroine's beauty and the words of the magically powerful 'donor' Falada, related to and then observed by the king. The villain is then exposed and punished, and the heroine becomes queen. The invariable pattern of folktale, observed by Propp, is there: misfortune, followed by a struggle which results in a victory for the protagonist; and the consequence of this victory, which is recognition of the protagonist as triumphant and splendid. This kind of analysis may not explain the strange features of the story, but it is illuminating in that it liberates us from detail and interpretation in order to show us how to look for pattern and form.

Turning now to a consideration of the striking features of *The Goose-Girl*, its repetition of action and dialogue and its use of verse in dialogue give it a ritual quality: the action and dialogue at the stream are repeated twice, while the exchange with Falada's head and the heroine's secret dressing of her hair are repeated three times; the words 'If this your mother knew, her heart would break in two' are repeated six times, twice by the drops of blood, twice by Falada, once by the goose-boy and finally by the heroine herself. The adventure resembles more a formal dance than a heroine's struggle to prove her identity, and yet she proves it in the end. She puts up no overt resistance at all, except to arrange for Falada's head to be nailed beneath the gateway: indeed, her defencelessness before her waiting-maid is quite incredible, and her failure to attempt an appeal to the king or to her mother, or to the other attendants she must have had, is not at all explained by her extraordinary oath. There is no attempt in the story to imitate the measures we would resort to in actual life. The heroine does not assess the situation, weigh up the qualities of those she must deal with, or work out a strategy; the interest of the story does not lie in the tactical skill with which the heroine overcomes her enemy and convinces the king. Such skill involves employing a judgement and reasoning akin to those which we would employ in dealing with the external world, and it involves developing the characters with which the protagonist is dealing, describing how they are also engaged in making their own decisions and plans. Such a story, of which R. L. Stevenson's *Treasure Island* is an example, has the reader engaging in the adventures with all these tactical skills, working out with the hero how he might deal with the situations arising.

A moment spent with Jim Hawkins, hero of *Treasure Island*, would be of value here. Jim finds himself alone on a drifting ship with his enemy Israel Hands; he is a child, unable to sail the ship, and Hands is a wounded sailor. Hands finds a pretext to get Jim below deck, so that he can secretly collect a knife from another part of the deck; but Jim realizes this is a pretext and, pretending to go below, he watches Hands arm himself.

This was all that I required to know. Israel could move about; he was now armed; and if he had been at so much trouble to get rid of me, it was plain that I was meant to be the victim . . . Yet I felt sure that I could trust him in one point, since in that our interests jumped together, and that was in the disposition of the schooner. We both desired to have her stranded safe enough, in a sheltered place, and so that, when the time came, she could be got off again with as little labour and danger as might be; and until that was done I considered that my life would certainly be spared.[9]

Jim sails the ship under Hands' instructions, and, absorbed in his task of beaching her in the North Inlet, he realizes only just in time that the moment has come when Hands will knife him. The two characters are both engaged in anticipating moves, outwittings, trickery and the planning of strategies. The world of such a story, however unlikely it might be, is one in which our reasoning powers can and must operate; the laws by which it works approximate to those of the observed external world. In *The Goose-Girl* there are none of these enjoyments, and yet the story's survival in oral tradition, before the Brothers Grimm recorded it, suggests that it has something to offer.

The reader might object here once again, saying that a popular folktale could not be compared usefully with a great work of literature, and that we must expect the two stories to be wholly different in kind. My point is that what we find in the folktale is exactly what we find anywhere in literature where magical fantasy has become engaged in creating fiction: in folktale we may find the fantasy structure in its pristine form, obscured very little or not at all by the transforming work of the intellect and imagination, and an examination of it here will isolate its distinguishing features.

Certain structural features are evident from a position outside the story, but from this position the story can easily be misunderstood or distorted. It would be easy to assume that this is an Oedipal story, with its king and queen in separate kingdoms and its 'young king', who reigns with his bride at the end of the story, without there being any mention of the death of the old king. Thoughts of power might also seem to be present as the princess sets out armed with the drops of blood which give her power. However, it is also possible to see from a position outside the story that its conflict is between the princess and the waiting-maid. From a position outside the story, one might discern aspects of the story's content, without seeing all and without seeing the relative importance of the elements. The story might also be interpreted in fragments rather than understood as a coherent whole. In order to understand the story as a coherent whole, one has to recognize the nature of the thought creating it.

The conflict makes little sense to outward view, the villain having inexplicable powers of villainy and the princess inexplicable lack of power, especially for a princess. The villain uses no strategies, merely assuming power 'just like magic', while the princess loses power 'just like magic', and then regains it by magic rather than by strategy. In fact, magic is ubiquitous in the story: where is it coming from? If one takes identification of storyteller and audience with the protagonist to its logical conclusion, it will become apparent that the heroine (storyteller and audience) is making this story up and the magic is all coming from her. She is thinking magically. Let us move inside the story and join the heroine to test this notion.

Having moved inside the story, I assume that every detail is important, for the details have been preserved in oral tradition and would not have been remembered had they not been important to the sense of the story. I also examine every detail in its context: for example, the blood and the horse mean in the story what the text tells us they mean, and if there is no contextual information (as in the case of the iron-stove later in the story), there can be no reliable interpretation. Researches into folklore, social anthropology and psychoanalysis as to the meaning of blood and horses can only produce speculations which tell us little about this particular story. I shall begin my analysis by examining the ritually repeated material, because this is likely to be the most significant detail.

The six-times spoken 'If this your mother knew, her heart would break in two' must be the most important words of the story. They are spoken twice by the drops of the queen's blood given to the heroine, afterwards to be lost, twice by the beheaded horse, once by the goose-boy to the king (quoting the horse), and then, finally, by the heroine herself. This stresses the importance of the mother's love and support in the story, and a progression in the heroine's conviction that she has this love and support. The heroine also performs the action by the stream twice: the waiting-maid's refusal to fetch water in the golden cup, the drinking from the stream and the blood's ritual words expressing the mother's love and support. She then performs three times the action at the king's palace: the beheaded Falada's assurance that she is a princess, the ritual words expressing the mother's love and support, and the secret combing and braiding of the hair, having commanded the wind to draw the goose-boy away. The events rehearsed twice seem to express the heroine's overwhelming feeling that she is not a princess, and after the second rehearsal the drops of blood, expressing the mother's love and dismay, fall away without her even noticing, leaving the heroine powerless. Meanwhile, the waiting-maid gains power, not through gaining the drops of blood, but merely through the heroine's lack of them. It seems that the power rests in the assurances of the mother's love and desire that she should become a queen; once she loses those assurances, she loses all sense of being a princess. It can be seen that the earlier interpretation that the drops of blood express the queen's power is not quite correct: they express the heroine's feeling that her mother wishes her to be a queen, and it is this that gives her power. Why does she not even notice the loss of the drops of blood? We are told that her anxiety prevents her from doing so, which seems to mean that she forgets them and all that they express in her overwhelming sense that she is not a princess. A usurper is the cause of her plight: a usurper, wishing to marry the prince, is the cause of the heroine's loss of her sense of being a princess. The conflict seems to be between the heroine's feeling that she is on her way to becoming a queen, with her mother's love and approval, and her accompanying feeling that she is a usurper. During the twice-performed action, her feeling that she is a usurper gains the upper hand.

The events rehearsed three times first feature the encounter with the severed head of Falada. Why is the assurance of the queen's love, silenced with the loss of the drops of blood, to return only in the words of the severed head of the horse? It is noteworthy that the horse has nothing to say until it is a severed head: why did it not speak by the stream, refusing to carry the waiting-maid to the prince, and why did it not speak on arrival at the king's palace? Why, too, does the princess not pay to have the horse saved rather than the head? The heroine has had the horse beheaded and so revived the assurances that she is a princess and that her mother would grieve that she has become a goose-girl. With the third rehearsal the king's attention is drawn to this evidence. The threefold sequence is a particularly difficult part of the story. The heroine is clearly engaged in making an indirect appeal to the king, arranging for its events to come to his knowledge, and the second part of the threefold sequence, the secret dressing of her golden hair, might throw light on the first. An interesting elaboration in one translation[10] of the heroine's charm song to the wind helps to bring out some of the latent material in the story, as alterations often do[11]: the princess sings that she will plait her 'gold' hair 'in a crown'. After each encounter with the severed head, the heroine seems to be secretly treating herself as a queen. There has been a change of feeling in the story which may have to do with the beheading of the horse.

A less obvious repetition, this time contrastive, can be seen in the waiting-maid's usurping the golden cup, to which the heroine yields, and the goose-boy's attempts to usurp the golden strands of hair, which the heroine resists. Similarly, the queen's help in the drops of blood is of no avail, as the heroine gives in to the waiting-maid, while the old king's help is achieved through the heroine's resisting the goose-boy and causing him to complain to the king. Furthermore, while the heroine loses the drops of blood altogether, she arranges that Falada will speak the same words for her – and, furthermore, herself speaks the words of the blood and the horse on the sixth occasion that they appear, when they are followed by the recognition of the king. These parallels make more evident the contrast between the action which is performed twice and that which is performed three times: the heroine seems to be contemplating the same feelings twice over, in a different mood on each occasion.

Falada and his fate are central to the story. The horse's name may be connected with that of Roland's horse Veillantif or Valentine, while one version of the story calls him simply 'Folle', meaning 'Fohlen', foal.[12] It is his role to bear the heroine (whether princess or usurper) to the place where she is to become queen, and it is also his role to express the heroine's right to be queen – once he is beheaded and not before. The first role he carries out by bearing the usurper to the prince and this must be the reason for his second role, being beheaded as a consequence of bearing the usurper to the prince. The beheading act gives the heroine the ability to make herself queen, for it speaks her right to be queen, proclaiming her mother's support at the gateway to her kingdom, and each time it does so, the heroine treats herself as a queen, this very behaviour gaining the attention of the king. Conrad repeats the ritual words and then the heroine is able to speak them herself so that the king hears them. The beheading probably expresses the heroine's punishment of her usurping thoughts and perhaps, too, a demonstration of the reduction of that propulsion towards the kingdom which Falada has expressed. This last would be in tune with the low profile adopted by the heroine during the threefold action sequence, in contrast to the role of the aggressive usurper which the heroine has seen herself playing and has now dealt with. It is worth recording here that in some versions of the story the heroine herself is mutilated[13]; alternative versions, like the seeming alterations of translators, remain faithful to the story.[14]

An examination of the repeated events in the story suggests that the story develops as a conflict between the heroine's feelings and ends when the conflict is resolved. The heroine's prime desire seems to be to achieve a sense that she is a queen, the recognition she seeks being fundamentally self-recognition. There does not seem to be a desire to oust her mother, who is presented throughout as lovingly supporting her; the heroine's chief desire where her mother is concerned is to retain a feeling that she has her support, and, significantly, she repeats the ritual words expressing her mother's love and support just as she is bringing about her status as queen. The usurper probably enters into the story because the heroine confuses becoming a queen with taking her mother's place. Incestuous feelings do not seem to be prominent in the story: the heroine seems to be more interested in reigning over a kingdom, the detail with which the story ends. Another notable point is that the elimination of the usurper is not necessary for the heroine's triumph, which is achieved by the activities in the threefold sequence: the heroine punishes and disposes of her usurping self, but she has already attained her feeling of being a queen, through a ritual involving punishment. Finally, the iron-stove, which the heroine uses as a confidant, may be no more than a convention employed by the heroine, since a stove is often a confidant in folktale[15]; it may at some time have meant more, but, whatever is the case, there is too little contextual information for any certainty as to what it expresses in this story.

Structurally, it can be seen that the heroine begins with an initial situation in which she feels she is a princess, the loved daughter of a queen, who sends her off to her kingdom. She sets out into another situation; I call this situation a second 'move', using Propp's word but with a rather different meaning.[16] A second 'move', over and above the initial move, is, according to my definition, a re-enactment of the feelings expressed in the initial move, thinking over these feelings afresh in a different mood. In this second move, the heroine loses her feeling that she is a princess, supported by her mother, being overwhelmed by the feeling that the girl on her way to becoming a queen is a usurper. The conflict in this move is acted out twice. The heroine then passes into a third move, in which she deals with the conflict that has arisen. Here, she is a goose-girl with a secret determination to become a queen, and in this longer, more complex move she acts out her feelings afresh and achieves a resolution, establishing her feeling that she is a queen. The conflict in this move is rehearsed three times, and some of its detail parallels detail in the second move significantly.

The Goose-Girl is the invention of its heroine and those who join her by participating in her story, and its subject matter is her conflicting feelings, her wish to be splendid and significant opposed by her fears; the conflict between these emotions propels the story as the heroine acts them out, thinking magically. She contemplates her wishes and feelings and these thoughts take form spontaneously as her characters, her deeds and her experiences. The characters of a magical fantasy have no separate existence from the hero: they are either the hero himself, acknowledged (like the princess in *The Goose-Girl*) or unacknowledged (like the usurping waiting-maid), or they are other people about whom he is thinking, their attributes expressing, not characteristics observed with a recognition of their 'otherness', but how the hero feels about himself or what he wishes for himself. The queen and king are loving and fair-minded, respectively, towards the heroine of *The Goose-Girl* because she wishes them to be loving and fair-minded; if she felt hostility towards them she might represent them as a witch and an ogre. Fantasy dwells on parent figures a great deal, probably because they are important in our primal experience and fantasy is primitive. Of course, kings and queens in fantasy have no political reality: they are images, expressing parental or other authority figures, or a vision the protagonist has of him- or herself. A heroine will be a princess, a waiting-maid, a goose-girl or a queen according as to how she feels about herself.

A magical fantasy takes shape in moves, which arise from changes of mood as the protagonist contemplates his feelings, or from a desire to deal with conflict by using fresh means. Fantasy also makes frequent use of ritual action and language, which can have extra magical force, like magic words or objects: the six-times spoken 'If this your mother knew, her heart would break in two' will have some of the force of magic words, helping to give power to the heroine's wish to have this maternal support. A protagonist may seek to bind and reinforce one of his wishes in this way to give it power over opposing feelings.[17] Similarly, the threefold performance of the crucial action in the third move of *The Goose-Girl* may have a magic power to resolve the conflict of the story. Fantasies very often take on the character of a magical rite, through which protagonists and participants bring about wishes and solutions to conflicts.[18] The ritual quality of fantasy may have other purposes also: its playfulness gives pleasure and may even help to disguise the exact nature of the feelings achieving expression. Furthermore, when a fantasy is being transmitted in oral tradition, ritual repetition and shaping of the material of the story will act as a mnemonic.

Disguise is another important characteristic of magical fantasy, concealing any details which tellers and listeners prefer to have concealed. The heroine of *The Goose-Girl*'s splitting off the usurper from herself acts as a disguise, but this splitting up of the heroine can be seen to be mainly because of its dramatic usefulness, facilitating the enactment of the heroine's conflicting feelings. The prince and the king in *The Goose-Girl* play what amounts to a single role, the young king's introduction probably being to disguise the idea of marrying the father, which arises as the heroine thinks of being a queen and which leads to the conflict about being a usurper. The parent figures, the queen and king, are, as so often in fantasy, split up, appearing in separate moves, for the dual purposes of disguise and play.

It is evident from the study of *The Goose-Girl* that a useful initial clue to the presence of a fantasy is the kind of questions which a work raises. These questions might also be raised by some great works of literature. In the case of the question raised in my Preface, 'Why isn't Hamlet king?', if no convincing reason why Hamlet has not been made king can be found at the verbal level of the play, perhaps there may be a fantasy structure, underlying the verbal level, in the midst of which Hamlet's not being king makes sense. However, absurdities in these works tend to be ignored, entire attention being given to the author's imaginative treatment of his fantasy material. The problem is that the two levels of thought are totally distinct and we tend to acknowledge the existence of only one of them. Meanwhile, the activity of fantasy may not only be unacknowledged: paradoxically, it is also so familiar that we tend not to notice its absurdities.

It should be stressed that this inquiry has no biographical purpose. I do not believe that the discovery of a fantasy structure in works by Rider Haggard, Charlotte Brontë, H. C. Andersen and Shakespeare presents us with reliable evidence as to the personalities of these particular writers. To take *Jane Eyre* as an example, the fantasy structure in that novel is expressed with power, but its themes are familiar in tradition and recent literature, and in as far as the material might give expression to the author's own experience, its commonplace nature prevents it from telling us anything remarkable about her. Fantasy material is, to a great extent, common property; only in cases where a fantasy fails to achieve general acceptance might we ask whether the author has expressed unusual – and therefore revealing – fantasies in it. I must add that it cannot be claimed for the great writers that they have imaginatively used a fantasy structure without their own magical thought being involved, for the imagination could not create or re-create a fantasy structure in its entirety, skilled as it might be, at times, in handling fragments of fantasy.

As this is an inquiry into the nature and behaviour of magical fantasy, certain important factors have to be placed, temporarily, in abeyance. Difference of literary genre and in the period of time to which a work belongs, is, in the main, ignored here. These factors categorize works of literature in a way that prevents critics from investigating and taking into account those deeper factors in the creative process which apply to all fiction. Another important matter which has to be suspended for the same reasons is difference in literary merit: weaknesses in the works studied will only be pointed out where they are relevant to the investigation. This decision to suspend critical discrimination is the reason why there has been no more concern with arranging the chapters according to the merit of their subjects than there has been with arranging them according to genre or date. The studies in this book are arranged so as to present the investigation clearly.

The choice of works to be studied has been made in order to explore magical storytelling as systematically as possible. Having illustrated a traditional fantasy in this Introduction, I shall explore how an individual author creates a fantasy in Rider Haggard's *She*. The chapter will show how the presentation of such a fantasy resembles and differs from the presentation of fantasy in oral tradition. In the next chapter, on Charlotte Brontë's *Jane Eyre*, there will be a study of a fantasy containing many moves, which is, nevertheless, much less obviously a fantasy than *She*, since the author's imaginative purposes have developed many of the moves. The third chapter, on H. C. Andersen's *The Ugly Duckling* and *The Shadow*, studies two further ways in which fantasy and imaginative art can relate to each other in a single work of fiction. In *The Ugly Duckling* they co-operate more completely than they do in *Jane Eyre*, and, in *The Shadow*, they operate quite separately: while lack of co-operation need not cause discord, it does so in *The Shadow*. The fourth chapter is devoted to exploring how 'fantasy' created by the imagination and by intellectual ingenuity differs from primitive fantasy, taking Tolkien's *The Lord of the Rings* as its example. Chapter Five studies Chaucer's *The Wife of Bath's Tale*, in order to examine how an individual author using a traditional fantasy may not re-create it faithfully or even only partly transform it: Chaucer totally transforms the fantasy for his imaginative purposes, so that its own purposes are eclipsed. Nevertheless, he depends upon his audience's memory of the fantasy for some of his effects. Chapter Six compares *Sir Gawain and the Green Knight* and *The Grene Knight* in order to explore how apparent alterations in surface detail, taking place during transmission, may not be expressing any real alteration in the fantasy, having remained faithful to it. The second part of this chapter compares *Sir Gawain and the Green Knight* with *The Lord of the Rings*, the two works both having the dual purpose of creating an adventure in a magical world and expressing a moral vision of human dilemma; the chapter shows how these works differ, since the magic in each has a different origin, that in *The Lord of the Rings* being intellectually contrived and that in *Sir Gawain and the Green Knight* being the magic inherent in primitive fantasy. The last chapter, on *Hamlet*, examines Shakespeare's treatment of his fantasy sources, this examination involving a study of his creative activity at the level of fantasy. Unlike Chaucer, Shakespeare does not totally transform the fantasy he uses; instead, he re-creates it faithfully, while, at the same time, making alterations to suit his dramatic purposes.

At the risk of being tedious, I begin some of my chapters with a little further explanation of the behaviour of fantasy in medieval romance, in order to clarify the discussion for those who have not read *Traditional Romance and Tale*.

1

She

This first chapter will consider H. Rider Haggard's romance *She*[1], in order to study how a fantasy may be presented in a work of individual authorship as opposed to a traditional story. *She* should show some of the characteristics of a fantasy which has not had to depend upon the general acceptance, comprehension and transmission of audiences for its preservation.

Many characteristics of traditional fantasy have already emerged in the tale of *The Goose-Girl*, but there needs to be a little more discussion of the genre before the study of *She*.

An essential feature of traditional fantasy is its linear form, which usually takes the hero or heroine from an initial situation of conflicting feelings, introduced either in the initial move or in the first two moves, to one or more places of adventure, where the protagonist struggles to resolve his conflicts. This place of adventure, which tends to be a longer move, may involve a fuller expression of the feelings in the initial situation and it is usually preceded by a journey, perhaps across a sea or a wilderness. In the medieval romances, in particular, this journey may be perilous, and it may express a state of exile. If the protagonist finds a resolution in his place of adventure, as does the heroine of *The Goose-Girl*, his story may end there, but in some stories the hero may transfer himself to a number of places of adventure, in each one dealing with his feelings afresh, before bringing about a victorious end to his story. The moves – those repetitions in the enactment of the central feelings of the story – are an essential morphological feature of traditional fantasy: occasionally a story has only one move, but most have two or three, while some medieval romances have six or more. In many stories the place of adventure which brings about the resolution is given mnemonic, ritual form through being divided into a threefold action sequence, as has already been observed in *The Goose-Girl*.[2]

Mnemonic, ritual form is an intrinsic feature of a story worn smooth by oral transmission. Moreover, every detail thus remembered must be important, taking its place in the coherent sequence of deeply meaningful pictures which is the story. Any attempts at transformation of this fantasy structure on the part of more rational levels of thought will do little more than provide rationalizations and, perhaps, seek to present the events of the story as having actually happened, in some far distant place or time. Rationalizations, where there are any, are likely to be brief, even casual, details which give reasons external to the fantasy, and appealing to our rational minds, for some of the events of the story. The information that the hero's father in *The King of the Golden Mountain*[3] is an impoverished merchant is such a detail: it only goes a small way to explain his listening to the absurd suggestion of the dwarf, which has its complete and quite different explanation at the level of fantasy. If *The Goose-Girl* included any rationalization, we might be told that the waiting-maid was the daughter of a rebel general, playing her part in his plot. It is rare for there to be such an instrusion as this on the part of rational thought, where a traditional fantasy is concerned, but in the work of individual writers it is common. While rationalizations are not at all in touch with the actual business of the fantasy concerned, this need not matter, as no explanations for the fantasy are required by those enjoying it; moreover, the explanatory material can provide additional enjoyment at another level of thought.

Several characters in a traditional fantasy may represent the hero, some of these doing so openly and others doing so in a more hidden way – either because they are disowned by the hero or because he has other reasons for keeping them separate from himself.[4] Characters other than the hero may be similarly split up into two or more characters. Among the hero's purposes in fragmenting character are the increased opportunities it gives for the play of his thoughts and the help it lends in disguising some of the thoughts of the story. In *The Goose-Girl* the heroine appears as both the princess and the waiting-maid, the more freely to act out her conflicting feelings.

Since the hero of a fantasy is thinking at a magical level, he has to find a solution to his conflicts by magical means. He may use objects, words or rituals which are invested with extra magical power, or he may achieve a transformation scene, in which he succeeds in changing his feelings – and thus his images – concerning a character in his story. In the case of a transformation scene, there is an abrupt change in the imagery expressing the character concerned, a change known as a shapeshift. Such a transformation takes place in *Beauty and the Beast*, where the heroine ceases to see a beast in her future sexual partner and sees a handsome prince, once she loves and wishes to marry the beast. The Loathly Lady story, appearing in the romance *The Weddynge of Sir Gawen and Dame Ragnell*[5], has a similar transformation scene, where the hero ceases to see an ugly bride, perceiving a beautiful one instead.

In turning now to *She*, it is first necessary to give a brief outline of the story. This cannot, of course, include all the detail which will be essential for the subsequent study. A university don named Holly, who narrates the story, finds himself the guardian of a child named Leo, and brings him up at his college, with the help of a manservant. He prefers to live apart from women. Leo is the only remaining representative of a family which can be traced back to an Egyptian priest of Isis, Kallikrates, in the third century B.C. When he is twenty-five years old, a mysterious chest left by his father is opened; it contains a letter from Leo's father, telling Leo of the quest of his family since the time of Kallikrates. Also in the chest is a potsherd, on which there is an account written by Amenartas, wife to Kallikrates, telling how Kallikrates was killed by a queen in Africa ' "... who is a magician having a knowledge of all things, and life and loveliness that does not die." ' This queen kills Kallikrates because he refuses to kill Amenartas and marry her. (In marrying Amenartas, he had broken his vows of priesthood.) Amenartas is addressing her son in her account, bidding him ' "seek out the woman and learn the secret of life" ' and also slay the woman, if he can, to avenge his father. However, messages on the potsherd reveal that no descendant of Kallikrates has succeeded in carrying out this bidding. The story of *She* is the story of how Leo, Holly and the manservant travel to Africa and seek out the queen. They have a perilous journey in a dhow to their destination on the East coast of Africa, and then they travel inland through marshes until they meet the Amahaggar, an African tribe. After several adventures among the Amahaggar, the heroes travel to Kôr, where 'She' lives, in the company of some of the Amahaggar, including Ustane, a girl in love with Leo. 'She' lives in the depths of the vast catacombs of Kôr, and when she sets eyes on Leo, she believes that he is his ancestor Kallikrates, returned to life. The heroes have a number of experiences at Kôr, among them the killing of Ustane by the jealous 'She'. Then 'She' takes them on the perilous journey to the pillar of fire, which can give Leo eternal life. This will prepare him for marriage with 'She'. Before Leo bathes in the pillar of fire, 'She' does so once more, to renew her life, but, instead, she withers into the old woman she really is, and dies. Leo and Holly manage to make the perilous journey back, eventually returning to their university.

In what ways does this story resemble traditional fantasies? Beginning with its morphology, there do appear to be some similarities. There are initial scenes set in the heroes' home, followed by a journey to a place where the heroes have a number of adventures. These adventures might or might not be found to divide up into several moves; nevertheless, they certainly culminate in a transformation scene. The end of the story is the feature most unlike a traditional fantasy, for it takes the form of an escape rather than a conquest.

However, an examination of a fantasy from a viewpoint outside it does not tell one much about it and can be misleading. Only a knowledge of *She* gained by participating in it and following its thought can determine whether it takes the form of a sequence of moves. Do the opening scenes in England express conflicting feelings on the part of the hero, and do the adventures in Africa relate to the situation in England as a struggle to solve its problems? If this turns out to be the case, the story is likely to be a creation of fantasy, like *The Goose-Girl*.

Treasure Island, while not a creation of fantasy, resembles a folktale in outward shape more decidedly than does *She*: it has opening scenes which might be an 'initial situation', a journey to a place of adventure, a struggle in the place of adventure and, finally, a conquest. It is experience of the story which shows that, while Jim Hawkins may be pitting his skills against adult men and thus acquiring a feeling that he has attained adulthood, the level of thought at which he is doing this is quite distinct from that of the heroine of *The Goose-Girl*. Jim's opponents are as much engaged in planning strategies as is Jim, so the story is hardly solipsistic and the focus is clearly on dealing expertly with a world akin to the external world.

On a superficial examination, it is the transformation scene of *She* which suggests that the story may have a fantasy structure. A transformation scene is obviously magical and it suggests that at least some of the thinking in *She* is magical. There are also a number of other features in the story which suggest a fantasy structure, since they are impossible in the external world. The information on the potsherd and the potsherd's survival within one family over a period of more than two thousand years are both impossible. Intriguingly, these impossibilities are presented with the help of some ingenious, intricate detail drawn from scholastic knowledge, a combination which might well occur in a fantasy of individual authorship. *She* abounds in rationalizations and protestations as to its actual truth, even with such remarks as 'notwithstanding that every page of this history must bear so much internal evidence of its truth, that obviously it would have been quite impossible for me to have invented it'.[6] If all the events of the story are history, the reader must ask how there could be a woman more than two thousand years old, why she, a white woman, is a queen in Africa, how one family can survive so long, handing down a fragile object, and why all this must be the centre of Leo Vincey's life two millenia later. An essential characteristic of fantasy – as opposed to stories such as *Treasure Island* – is that when we are no longer participating in the story we raise such questions as these about it.

If the hero is the creator of the story and thinking magically, then all the characters in the story are either himself or other people as he sees them when unable to perceive their 'otherness', being only concerned with his own feelings, wishes and needs. Many such feelings are infantile, although not necessarily so: as in *Beauty and the Beast*, fantasy can be seeking the attainment of emotional maturity. The potsherd's message concerns a woman with magical powers and an ancestor, and if we examine the attributes of 'She' and of the ancestor, it can be seen that they suggest a child's vision of parent figures, extraordinary as they are. 'She' is a queen and Kallikrates is the priestly forebear of the hero, who is confused with him. 'She' is described as wiser than Solomon, all-powerful, 'She-who-must-be-obeyed'[7], and a killer, but she is also a healing woman, healing Leo of his sickness, and her kiss is 'like a mother's kiss'.[8] She is, moreover, immortal and of immense age; there is a suggestion of death about her, as she lives in a tomb and looks like a corpse (we are told of her, 'Here's a corpse a-coming', she has a 'mummy-like form', and her 'garb . . . has a death-like air'[9]). The hero also invests her with a great beauty which makes her desired by all men who see her: this beauty expresses the hero's attraction to her; it is not the result of an aesthetic evaluation. The hero invests her, too, with no other interest but her love for himself: although wiser than Solomon and with the experience of two millenia, 'She' has but one occupation; she is waiting, waiting ' "for him I love" ' and he is the priest she killed who is born again in the hero. She loves Leo when she believes him to be the reincarnation of Kallikrates. The nature of the fantasy is becoming clearer and it can be seen that 'She' is true in a sense, within the limits of the hero's inner world, as he contemplates replacing his father. The answers to the questions the story raises begin to emerge: in particular, 'She' is a queen in Africa because she has the attributes and position of a queen in the hero's fantasy, and Africa, then so little known by Europeans – apart from its useful associations with adventure, mines, tombs, big game and mysterious black peoples – lent itself to an author already fascinated by the continent. Anything might be believed about the heart of the 'dark continent' in 1887, and the hero is presenting us with much to believe.

If the thinking appears tortuous, this is typical of fantasy. Examination of the quest reveals conflicting desires from the first. At the outset of the adventure, Leo is undertaking a quest which, according to the instructions of his ancestress Amenartas, was originally intended to avenge Kallikrates by slaying 'She' – having first discovered her secret of eternal life, so that he can then sit in the place of the pharaohs. This quest the hero does indeed perform, for he does slay 'She' in his transformation scene. There is also confusion as to whether or not Leo is Kallikrates, and this reflects confusion in the hero's mind. At the end of the story, Holly states his belief that Kallikrates and Leo are the same, while one also senses the separateness of Leo as he gazes at the corpse of Kallikrates.[10] 'She' says to Leo: ' "And thou, my Kallikrates, art the father, and in a sense thou art likewise the son" '.[11] A fundamental reason why Leo is so firmly proved the descendant of Kallikrates in the evidence of the potsherd emerges here.

A closer examination of the detail in the work shows further similarities with traditional fantasy. Most of the detail emerges as integral with the story's central feelings and purposes, engaged in giving expression to coherent sequences of thought at fantasy level. Where it is not, it is material taken from perceptions of the external world, and from historical and other learning, devoted to giving an illusion of actuality to the fantasy of the 'She' adventure. As the title suggests, the story is essentially about woman. At its outset the heroes live a life without women because women can, it is suggested, be cruel, dominant and apt to steal a man's child. Female cruelty is combined with beauty from the beginning, where a woman discards her lover, Holly, with the words, ' "... if I am Beauty, who are you?" ' The outset of the story also expresses a family, Holly playing the role of father, from which a mother is excluded. As *The Goose-Girl* suggests, it is a frequent feature of fantasy that the parental figures at the heart of the fantasy are split up: in *The Goose-Girl* the queen and king appear in separate moves, while in *She* the mother is absent but thought of in the first move, appearing in disguise in the second move (the place of adventure). The adventure is concerned with an approach to 'She' and then an escape. The hero's predominant wish is to live without her: he feels her fascination and allure, but he also wishes that these should be destroyed so that he can escape her. At the same time, he senses that the nature of the fascination being what it is, woman is ancient and dead, and he, in his attraction to her, is in danger of death. The exaggerated nature of the images is one of the hallmarks of fantasy. Their violent pictures express more fully the nature of the hero's thoughts than do Holly's words halfway through the story, saying that he wishes men could rest content to be apart from women, but he is not sure that they would be happy thus.[12]

Most of the great number of characters, events and other details in the story are images giving expression to the play of the hero's central preoccupations; the variety of detail links up to show just a few concerns. Among the Amahaggar, we learn that women are regarded as a source of life while fatherhood is not recognized and that a man may be eaten for scorning a woman; we also encounter a beautiful woman who is a corpse.[13] Later in the story, the hero's sense of the death surrounding 'She' is depicted in a variety of lurid imagery: of mummies, tombs, a heap of skeletons, a dance-drama depicting live burial, and corpses on fire – these last linking significantly with the destruction of Kallikrates' corpse and with the destruction of 'She' in the pillar of flame. At the verbal level, these details tend to be rationalized and presented as being about something other than what they are actually about. For example, the author describes the 'anthropophagous customs of the Amahaggar' and the embalming methods of the ancient people of Kôr (who 'injected fluid into' the 'veins', instead of using the disembowelling and brain-drawing method of the Egyptians [14]) as if this expedition were on a par with those of Livingstone and Burton. Such additional activity on the part of intellectual thought supports, rather than interferes with, the fantasy, since it lends an air of rationality to the magical themes of devouring and death.

In dealing with this material, one has to look for the principles behind the mass of detail, detail which includes rationalization. The statue of Truth, near the end of the story, is presented as concerned with the abstraction 'truth'. It takes the form of a beautiful, tenderly loving woman, naked except for a veil, and an inscription underneath says, 'There is no man born of woman who may draw thy veil and live, nor shall be. By Death only can thy veil be drawn, O Truth!'[15] As in the case of a traditional fantasy, this scene must be pictured: it is an image integral with the story's themes, expressing the hero's belief as to the truth about woman. The uncovered body reveals her attractions and the veil over her face hides who she is: death awaits him who draws the veil.

The points just made may be further illustrated by a closer examination of the characters. These all link up to show a fundamental concern with only three characters: 'She', the hero's priestly ancestor who is loved by 'She', and, thirdly, the hero, who is both distinct and not distinct from the priestly father-figure. Holly, who is given the role of narrator, is an aspect of the hero (an aspect contrasting with Leo in being unrequited lover of 'She'), while he also appears as a father, thus expressing the same confusion between father and son that we see in Leo and Kallikrates. Differences apparent between all the characters are due less to a development of them as individuals than to a splitting up of the fundamental characters in the hero's mind to give him more scope in the exploration of his fantasies. Sometimes the narrative enlarges on the character of 'She', having her speak at length, and, on those occasions, the fact that the author has two purposes at odds with each other – the purposes of the fantasy and also some aims at the level of imaginative art – becomes amusingly apparent. As Holly considers the evil nature of 'She', which is a projection of the hero's irrational fears as he contemplates her, he reflects that it probably springs from 'the natural cynicism which arises from age and bitter experience'.[16] The powerful mind and the wisdom, accumulated over two millennia, with which the hero invests 'She' are conveyed in trite comments such as the following on the ancient Greeks: ' "They were as beautiful as the day, and clever, but fierce at heart and fickle, notwithstanding." '[17] Holly also relates 'She' to the outer world of his time, contemplating her possible career as the usurper of absolute rule over the British Empire, making it the most 'glorious and prosperous' the world has ever seen, at the 'cost of a terrible sacrifice of life.'[18]

These features are a good example of what can happen when rational, imaginative thought sets to work on fantasy material without adequate control over the situation. An author may protest the reality of a fantasy creation as much as he wishes, because it is real at the level of fantasy; he may also link a world created by fantasy with aspects of the perceived external world because the two worlds are usually intermingled in our experience. But *She* is finally unsatisfying because the author's grasp of the fantasy is too uncertain. It is quite inappropriate treatment of 'She' to link the character with the political and intellectual areas of the external world. Her age, wisdom and power are attributes of a child's fantasy of a mother-figure, and a satisfactory development of her character would either be confined to that level of thinking or it would include an imaginative grasp of the content of the fantasy.

The culmination of the story is the transformation scene, and the context of a transformation scene is, of course, of prime significance: here the shapeshift takes place when the hero is to be made equal with 'She' in the flame of life, and then her husband and a king. These events are now made impossible. The young-looking, beautiful, seemingly immortal, wise, powerful 'She' becomes old, ugly, dead, proved wrong, powerless. The heroes say that they still love her, but there is no real sense of loss, once our pity and amazement have passed. Instead, the exciting escape of the heroes engages the attention. It has really been a relief that 'She' has become transformed. At the moment when the hero is to be bound to 'She' for ever, he feels differently about her and thus sees her differently: feelings about her which were present before her transformation, but only subordinate, take over, eclipsing the former dominant ones. But transformation may not only be an expression of a change of feeling in the hero: in this story it seems also to be a wielding of magical power, an act invested with the ritual power to exorcise the vision of 'She' as desirable, as well as to destroy her, so that the hero's escape from all that 'She' represents to him is complete.

When one is studying any fantasy structure, even a fantasy structure worked on by the imagination, one must pay close attention to every detail and to its position in the sequence. However, a story which has not been passed down from one oral storyteller to another is likely to include features which are less urgently important, less clear, and less relevant to the fantasy themes, even at odds with them. There might be elaborations such as the detail on the potsherd and the extended conversations between Holly, Leo and 'She'; oral tradition would reduce such detail to essentials and present it in a more ritual form, so that the essentials might be more effectively committed to memory and easier to listen to. A possibility, also, in a story created by an individual author is the introduction of incidental interests – which is the likely explanation of the inclusion of the big game episodes, although one cannot be certain that these do not carry further meaning. If they do not, it is likely that they would be dropped in oral tradition. If *She* were a traditional fantasy one would have to assume that all the details of the obstacles on the journey to the flame of life, and the escape from it (those including the spur and the rocking stone), link up to form a meaningful picture – for otherwise they would not be remembered. As it is, the obstacles may have been imaginatively invented each in their turn to give readers an account of a journey fraught with hardship and thrilling danger. This, however, does not rule out the possibility that the details describe a fantasy picture, conveying thoughts of a particular danger in this adventure with 'She', at the same time as they describe the thrilling journey and escape. Perhaps only some of the obstacles are images. In a work of this kind, one must be ready both to spot the activity of magical thought, and also to find that it gives place at times to other levels of thought, even at the heart of the story. This last would be unlikely to occur in a fantasy in oral tradition.

It might be further observed that the imaginative thought apparent in *She* is not concerned with transforming parts of the fantasy so that aspects of the outer world are sharply and tangibly evoked, locations sensuously realized and characters convincingly quickened into life. When Rider Haggard describes the African scenes, these descriptions are drawn from fantasy, not from the observation which he has been in a position to make. The location chosen for his story (now Mozambique and, possibly, Malawi) does not even resemble the South Africa he knew. The location itself was little known in 1887, when *She* was first published – although Dr Livingstone had explored parts of it, published his record and died, and Sir Harry Johnstone was busy in the area. Rider Haggard would not amaze many people by presenting the area as one of swamp and extinct volcano, covered with the remains of an Egyptian-style civilization; and clearly he deliberately chose an area known to exist but which could be freely described by fantasy. It is significant that the marsh scene in the story bears no particular resemblance to an African marsh – as it might be personally observed or as it might be created from a study of Livingstone's writings. Its water is described as 'peaty'[19] (not a tropical phenomenon) and there is no suggestion of the large, unique, very striking bird populations which characterize these areas. While the nature of a writer's activity in one work cannot be an indication of his activity in another, it is interesting to note that, in Rider Haggard's *King Solomon's Mines*, the landscape bears no resemblance to that of its supposed location in Africa (where the Kalahari Desert extends westward into the Namib), but it does bear a distinct resemblance to a woman's body. The heroes struggle over a desert, reaching at last the thirst-quenching, nourishing area of Sheba's breasts, and then pass over the fair land to a horseshoe-shaped, flat-topped hill outside Loo, before finally going down to King Solomon's mines. This is a particularly striking example of how fantasy may create a landscape; in *She* the imagery is more complicated, but the landscape and characters powerfully convey the hero's conflicting emotions concerning 'She'.

In conclusion, it appears that *She* is composed of a fantasy structure and also of additional material, subordinate to the aims of the fantasy structure, which is created by rational levels of thought. The peculiar linear progression of a fantasy structure is apparent, in that the adventures act out, to a conclusion satisfying to the hero, the feelings in the initial situation. A sharp difference between *She* and traditional stories is that *She* does not culminate in a 'victory'; the transformation scene does not express a change in the hero's feelings about 'She' similar in kind to the change expressed in the transformation scenes of *Beauty and the Beast* and *The Weddynge of Sir Gawen and Dame Ragnell*. While Beauty and Sir Gawain make what has seemed ugly beautiful, through overcoming such feelings as fear, the hero of *She* brings about the reverse transformation, because such feelings as fear have taken over. The transformation scene in *She* may or may not be idiosyncratic, but, in general, fantasy which has not had to depend upon acceptance in popular tradition may sometimes be idiosyncratic rather than common currency.

Another notable difference between *She* and a traditional story is that oral tradition has not shaped and smoothed off the work into mnemonic, ritual form. It remains in the memory afterwards as largely a jumble of events and detail, even while two, not very distinct, moves, divided by a sea journey, may be discerned, in which there is a repetition of the hero being both attracted and repelled by women and escaping from them. The content of the second move is somewhat repetitive and cyclical in character, but the repetitions have no distinct and shapely form. This is a far cry from *The Goose-Girl*, with its clearly separated moves and its twofold and threefold action sequences within the second and third moves. The character of the repetitions in *She* – compared with the formal action sequences of *The Goose-Girl* – also arises from the story's lack of ritual purpose, a lack confirmed by the character of the transformation scene. *She* is an indulgence in a dream, the hero using ritual only to destroy the dream when he feels it has gone far enough; there is no attempt to explore and resolve conflict.

The study of *She* has shown, too, that a fantasy created by an individual author may differ from a traditional fantasy in containing material which is not essential to its magical purposes; such material would be dropped in oral transmission, because it would be forgotten. Rider Haggard's imagination, moreover, has been very active as he has presented the fantasy of *She*, and this has produced effects amusingly at odds with it and sometimes destructive of its power. There is also the possibility, in a fantasy of individual authorship, that the author's imaginative purposes have been engaged in creating some of the scenes rather than magical thought: in a non-traditional story, one cannot expect to find a wholly coherent fantasy structure.

I shall now turn to Charlotte Brontë's *Jane Eyre*, in order to study a fantasy structure which has many more moves than has *She*, and also to give attention to a work which is much less obviously a fantasy than *She*, since the author's imaginative purposes have transformed many of the moves. In *Jane Eyre* fantasy and imagination operate together in harmony.

2

Jane Eyre

This discussion of *Jane Eyre*[1] will be mainly concerned with tracing the numerous moves of the novel's fantasy framework, and it is therefore necessary to begin by giving further attention to the behaviour of the multi-move fantasy.

The multi-move fantasy is commonly found among the medieval romances, where the hero may repeat his enactment of his conflicts over and over again, varying his approach as he explores them and seeks a resolution. We may sometimes be aware of our thinking in such a cyclical fashion when we are seeking the solution to a problem in everyday life. For example, when we have to confront someone about something, we may mentally act out how this may be done, not once but many times, trying out one way and then another, often changing our mood, until we are finally satisfied with a particular method. Of course, in these circumstances, we would be wise to be thinking rationally, while the moves I am concerned with in this study are created by magical thought. Magical moves are invisible to rational thinking, but when the magical thought creating the story concerned is followed accurately, the parallel cycles of thought concerning the central feelings of the story may emerge as the most striking feature of its structure. The best example of the multi-move romance is *King Horn*[2], because it is the most clear-cut, and I shall discuss it briefly here, while a fuller discussion of it may be found in *Traditional Romance and Tale*.[3]

King Horn has six moves. The hero transfers himself to a different place for each one, crossing water in order to do so, and arriving in a different guise, once with a change of name, to express the fresh mood in which he approaches his conflicts. Each place of adventure contains a king, a woman and the hero. In his first move he is a prince with the aggressive name 'Horn', who arranges that his father should be killed and he himself exiled. In his next move he is a thrall at the court of another king, who loves the king's daughter and arranges that he should be exiled again because this love is a threat to the king. He arrives in disguise at another court for his third move, this time as 'Goodmind', and here he saves the king from the monstrous giant (himself) that wishes to destroy him; afterwards he renounces the princess offered as a reward. For his fourth move he returns to the court and princess of the second move as a beggar, but he is no longer afraid of the king and calls himself 'Horn' unashamedly. In his fifth move he returns to his initial, home situation and makes himself king, intending to return afterwards to claim the princess. Finally, in his last move, disguised as a harper, he eliminates the character who, in seeking to take the princess by force from her cowed father, embodies his own feeling that he is committing theft in taking the princess. Having exorcised all feeling that he is doing wrong, he marries the princess and can end his story.

King Horn exemplifies many morphological features recurrent in traditional fantasy. Particularly to be noted here is the similarity between the way its hero treats the beginning of his story and the way the heroine of *The Goose-Girl* treats the beginning of hers. The hero is a prince called 'Horn' in his first move, planning to make himself a king without saying so. He then sets out on this quest and, in a second move, acts out his feelings more explicitly, this time appearing as a thrall whose love for the princess at this second court is a threat to the king, necessitating a further move to resolve these problems and achieve his aims. While the central feelings of the fantasy are more explicitly expressed in the second move, they are also more disguised, the court at which it takes place being presented as another court rather than home. The heroine of *The Goose-Girl* similarly begins her story as a princess on her way to becoming a queen, and, having set out, similarly takes on lowly status, the aspirations of the initial move being seen as those of a usurper; a third move – a place of adventure – is created for the resolution of this conflict. In a number of traditional fantasies the second move takes the form of a sojourn in a humble, loving home, which expresses another way in which the hero sees, and wishes to see, the parental characters involved in the central feelings creating the story.[4] Another interesting feature in *King Horn* is the last move, following the triumphant move in which the hero achieves his sense of being a king: it is created because making himself king has not been enough to give him the feeling that he may marry the princess; he still feels that he is seizing her from the king, and this feeling has to be exorcised before he can marry his princess and end his story. In the Grimm story of *The Golden Bird*[5], there are two such moves following the triumphant move, one in which the hero seeks to punish and dispose of his thieving aspect through arranging for his brothers to be punished, and a further one, created because the hero finds no resolution in such self-deceit, in which he undergoes a deeply disguised ritual of self-punishment, thus finding forgiveness for his unacknowledged self.

In the following study I shall explore how far *Jane Eyre* shows these characteristics of traditional fantasy in addition to the imaginative art which we expect in a novel. *Jane Eyre* appears to have a complete, multi-move fantasy structure underlying the entire novel, which has been transformed in many parts by the activity of the novelist. As I have pointed out in my Preface, one is struck by the novel's strange coincidences and repetitions. One of these occurs when Jane Eyre arrives among a household of unknown cousins who parallel the cousins at the beginning of the novel: in each case, there are a male and two female cousins, the male cousins called respectively John Reed and St John Rivers. There are three striking parallels here: in family pattern, in the name 'John' (the 'St' being an appropriate addition) and in the surnames, which are linked in idea. While imaginative art may also adopt repetition to express its purposes, these particular repetitions are too like those peculiar to fantasy not to invite investigation. There is also a strange exile between the leaving of Mr Rochester and the arrival at the Rivers' house, which is reminiscent of medieval romance: while the hardships of this exile are evoked with poignant realism, the realistic treatment cannot make this wandering without any destination, eventually to make an amazing arrival, any less extraordinary.

The exile, the dreamlike arrival and the apparent parallels suggest that the novel takes the form of a series of moves, the heroine transferring herself from one place of adventure to another, in each one dealing with her feelings afresh, until she brings about a happy end to her story. It might be argued that the work has eight moves, some more obvious in structure than others: the initial move at Gateshead; the second move at Lowood; the third, a meeting with someone from Gateshead, readjusting the heroine's relationship to that situation; the fourth at Thornfield; the fifth at Gateshead; the sixth at Thornfield; the seventh at Moor House and Morton, and the eighth at Ferndean. While there is room for disagreement as to whether the third move is distinct from the second and whether the fifth is distinct from the fourth and sixth, it would be difficult to deny the presence of these moves. But there is, of course, no reason why a novel should not take the form of a sequence of cycles of thought and still be imaginative art. Only a close examination of the recurring content of *Jane Eyre* reveals that the story's fundamental framework is the creation of fantasy, technically the creation of the heroine, Jane Eyre. Charlotte Brontë's work as an imaginative artist is, structurally, a development of the situations and characters in the fantasy framework through the employment of imaginative thought taking place concurrently with magical thought.

The eight moves all repeat the heroine's desire to readjust her estimation of her own size in relation to that of others. She is haunted by a sense of her own smallness and feels the need to convince herself repeatedly of her powers. Because she feels small, she feels a difficulty in obtaining the love and esteem of others, and she also feels that her desire to win the love of others conflicts with her desire to possess her own self. Her need for love, security and esteem is great. As she passes from move to move, seeking a sense of being both loved and an independent individual, the conflict between these two desires is increased by a further conflict between them, and this fresh conflict plays a part in propelling the story forward. The heroine's desire for a sense of her own ascendancy and independence becomes threatened by her association of love and security with the love of parents. Thus, when she thinks of marriage, she thinks of a father-figure, and this reinforces her sense of her childlike dependence and its accompanying urge to secure love with submission. Her thoughts of a fatherly husband also leave her with a confused fear that she is seeking to marry her father (which she may, in part, be doing), and this fear plays an important role in the conflict.

In the initial move, at Gateshead, the heroine is in the unsatisfactory home situation typical of traditional fantasy. The heroine sees herself as an unloved poor relation, cruelly and unjustly treated by an aunt by marriage, Mrs Reed, and by her children, John, Elizabeth and Georgiana. She sees herself as undersized, she is frightened of everyone, yet has aspirations, and the details of the move all express these feelings. Her world, in her initial move, seems to be populated by 'tower-like' people and 'diminutive' people. At first, she enjoys such a world as it is portrayed in *Gulliver's Travels*, but the book's giants come to seem 'gaunt goblins' and its 'pigmies malevolent and fearful imps'; Gulliver comes to be seen as 'a most desolate wanderer in most dread and dangerous regions'. Her future headmaster, Mr Brocklehurst, who visits the house, is like a 'black pillar', while the heroine's one object of love is her doll, a 'miniature scarecrow'. Her role in the family is lowly to the extent that she carries out the tasks of an under-nurserymaid. Those around her bully and condemn her; if John hits her, everyone takes his side. Even the deceased uncle, who had kindly taken her in as a baby, is a cause of terror: Jane fears his ghost. Meanwhile, she enjoys reading stories of love and adventure, and is fascinated by lurid pictures depicting terror and death. She is also concerned with fighting the enemies by whom she feels she is surrounded and with learning how to win. Before leaving Gateshead, she speaks her mind fully to her aunt about her wrongs and feels herself to be the 'winner in the field', elated but also frightened by her 'hated and hating position'. The feelings in this initial move, however reasonable they might seem to us as the experiences of a child, are contemplated at the level of fantasy. It is the heroine's feelings about herself, her small self-image, her lack of self-esteem and her failure to be on her own side which create the hostile ogres around her.

The author's imagination has, however, also been at work. Much of the emotional experience giving rise to the story is evidently explored from the points of view of all the characters involved. Jane ponders on the reasons why her situation at Gateshead is so unhappy and decides that she is by nature so opposite to the Reed family that it has not been possible for a spontaneous sympathy to grow up between them. The scene in which she speaks her mind to her aunt shows a novelist's psychological insight: Mrs Reed is frightened and tries to find ways of coping with an angry child, but her resources take her only as far as a suggestion that Jane returns to the nursery to lie down. Afterwards, Jane's elation is followed quickly by a frightened urge to ask Mrs Reed's pardon, which she quells because she knows it would only give rise to a 'repulse . . . with double scorn'. Just before she leaves Gateshead, Jane stands up to Bessie, the nurse, in an entirely different way: she simply tells Bessie lovingly that she must not scold, and her new 'frank and fearless' manner changes Bessie's manner; they part as friends. Here there is a penetrating consideration of the forces that give rise to bullying: a 'frank and fearless' manner brings out a friendly and understanding response in others, while those who are afraid of people, withdrawn and hard to fathom, provoke hostility in others.

The fantasy creating the initial move is worked over by the novelist's powers of empathy and rational scrutiny. The result is a quite convincing presentation of a child experiencing the fantasy world all children experience, and in the process of learning how to perceive the outer world, how to turn the ogres into real people and thereby engage in creative relationships with them.

The transfer to the second move, Lowood School, arises immediately from the heroine's angry words to Mrs Reed: 'Send me to school soon . . . for I hate to live here'. The suggestion of the boarding school is first assigned to the kindly apothecary, Mr Lloyd, while the heroine welcomes it because she wishes to learn; 'school would be a complete change: it implied a long journey, an entire separation from Gateshead, an entrance into a new life'. The journey she then makes into the second move is undertaken on her own, through cold, 'rain, wind and darkness', a journey reminiscent of the lonely, frightening journeys of medieval romance.

The account of Jane's life at Lowood School is the most realistic part of the novel, and it is created from the author's direct experience of a school of its type. This realism penetrates deeper than the stark details of the physical hardships, the teaching methods and the almost interminable moralizing of a girls' boarding school in the nineteenth century: it penetrates to realities which people of all epochs must recognize. The Lowood scenes evoke the frustration, insecurity and humiliation of being a child, the victim of the misunderstanding of adults, subject to their authority and yearning for their sympathy.

However, the role of this part of the novel as a move in the heroine's fantasy can also be discerned. The move follows the pattern of many a medieval romance in expressing a contrasting vision of the home situation from that expressed in the initial move. In medieval romance the hero may transfer himself to a second home with humble, loving parents, while, in *Jane Eyre*, the heroine's physical circumstances are humbler, this hardship offset by the loving care of the superintendant, Miss Temple. The very name 'Lowood' may be significant, as names often are in romance; 'Gateshead' and 'Thornfield' may be equally significant place names, while 'Miss Temple' may be another significant name. A link can be seen between the roles of Mrs Reed and Miss Temple, Mrs Reed being in the position of maternal guardian to the heroine in the first move and Miss Temple taking up this position, in practice, in the second; neither is a complete, fully rounded character, Mrs Reed being only bad and Miss Temple only good. 'Cardboard' characters may simply be the work of a bad novelist, but they may also be a sign that fantasy is at work, for fantasy tends to split up personality, its different aspects being represented by different characters. Mr Brocklehurst's fantasy role is that of a contrasting father-figure to the kindly, deceased uncle in the first move: the heroine does not give herself good, effective fathers in the initial moves (unless Mr Lloyd be one), and Mr Brocklehurst is seen as one who not only crushes the heroine's sense of her importance and her rights, but also as one who, in ordering the hair of fellow pupils to be cut off, seeks to destroy her power.

A third important character is Helen Burns, another pupil, who is solitary, serious and intellectual like Jane, but of a humble, accepting and deeply religious nature, unlike the rebellious, questioning heroine, yearning for the love of other human beings. A consideration of the discussions between Jane and Helen reveals both the work of fantasy and the treatment of the novelist. The novelist has presented through them the continual debate in a child's mind as to how much one should love adults and agree with their criticism, and how much one might hate and rebel against these adults, Jane arguing the case for rebellion and Helen for acceptance.[6] A later discussion between these two conveys a child's adjustment of her images of other people and herself: 'Mr Brocklehurst is not a god' and Jane need not be wholly and helplessly dependent on the love of other human beings.[7] Meanwhile, a consideration of the discussions between Jane and

Helen also leads one to see that Helen, who is not a complete personality, is an important aspect of the heroine at the level of fantasy, one that does not survive beyond this move: she is an ideal to be striven for, since she does not need to rebel; she does not doubt her own strength and independence, while Jane is rebelling against her own lack of these qualities.

The heroine completes her childhood in this second home, continuing her struggle at the level of fantasy for the attainment of a sense that she is taking her place in the world, and striving to cast off her feeling of being small and dependent. There then follows what appears to be a short move, in which the heroine contemplates herself in relation to her initial situation, readjusting her view; as this part of the novel is a complete reconsideration, albeit brief, of the heroine's central feelings creating the fantasy, it amounts to a separate move.

Bessie appears at Lowood School and brings Jane up to date with the situation at Gateshead, with which she has been wholly out of touch. Bessie pronounces her much cleverer but smaller than Eliza and Georgiana, and quite a lady. The Reed cousins have turned out badly, while the heroine is turning out well, and Mrs Reed is uneasy about John's bad conduct. Bessie also tells Jane that her uncle, Mr Eyre, had wanted to see her nearly seven years earlier; he looked quite the gentleman and was off to Madeira. Here the heroine regards herself in a much more favourable light in relation to her family than she had done in her first move, and with such thoughts she transfers herself to Thornfield.

Thornfield is the fourth move of the fantasy and the first place of adventure, where the heroine gives fuller expression to her central feelings and engages in a major struggle to achieve a resolution to her conflicts. The move corresponds to the heroine of *The Goose-Girl*'s adventure at the second palace. At Thornfield, the heroine meets Mrs Fairfax and Adèle: only gradually does she realize that they are not mother and daughter, and that Mr Rochester is the real owner of the house. This move has a dreamlike quality: it is entirely concerned with the fantasies of the heroine. Imaginative thought is mainly devoted to giving the concepts of fantasy an appearance (not very convincing) of being events actually taking place. Particularly dreamlike are the mysterious sounds indicating an unexplained presence, mysterious laughter, movements at night and the burning of Mr Rochester's bed in unexplained circumstances by a woman. One is left wondering why Jane remains in ignorance about the mad woman when every servant knows the secret. This factor is never satisfactorily rationalized and nor is the mad woman's continued presence in the house: it appears that the novelist who weighed the heroine's problems at Gateshead and Lowood has relaxed this critical vigilance and is allowing the story to emerge as a fantasy, making entire sense only at the level of magical thought. Some of the elements of the fantasy are reminiscent of childhood wonderings about parental behaviour at night, while the burning bed suggests more adult sexual imagery.

Accordingly, this discussion might be continued – for the present – as follows. As the heroine enters on this fourth move, her thoughts of herself appear to be linked with the character of Adèle. During the discussion about the 'cadeau', there is a suggestion of a comparison being made between Jane and Adèle by Rochester.[8] Adèle seems to be becoming Jane's opposite: frivolous, emotionally shallow, unintellectual. There are doubts as to whether or not Rochester is Adèle's father. The heroine, meanwhile, seems to be making Rochester formidable, while she stands up to him, not unlike a precocious child: ' "I don't think, sir, you have a right to command me merely because you are older than I, or because you have seen more of the world than I have . . ." '; Rochester says later: ' "Not three in three thousand raw school-girl governesses would have answered me as you have just done . . ." '. Rochester is forever referring to Jane as a 'child', 'little girl', 'elf', 'thing', 'pet lamb' and so forth. 'Elf' is commonly used to describe her: she is 'delicate and aerial' while she also sees herself as 'puny and insignificant'. All this, viewed as the creation of the heroine, suggests that she sees herself as a child, to some extent as Rochester's child, but she is a remarkably intelligent, attractive child. Rochester's manner towards her somewhat resembles that of an indulgent parent towards a favourite offspring: he is kind to her, while severe on others, and he behaves enigmatically towards her.

As the move proceeds, one is increasingly bewildered as to why Rochester is so extraordinarily equivocal towards Jane. That he should plan to marry her without divulging his married state is quite credible, but why all the pretence about Blanche Ingram? Why all the playing with Jane? Once again – as with the heroine's wonderings over the mysterious woman – we have a suggestion of the puzzled child, half aware of what the adults are up to and what they are saying, but not quite able to grasp it all. Jane has explained the mysterious woman by suspecting a quondam relationship between Rochester and Grace Poole, and now she believes there is also a relationship between him and Blanche Ingram. As she contemplates this man who has some of the characteristics of a father, the heroine sees him as being involved in a partly secret relationship with another woman, compared with whom she is only a child; she sees him as belonging to someone else. Blanche Ingram is strikingly like Bertha Mason in appearance, 'tall, dark, and majestic': Jane sees her married to Rochester in a charade, and in similarly vivid imagery visualizes Bertha Mason's relationship with Rochester. There is no empathy in the viewing of either character: one is reduced to a creature without the capacity for love and the other to a ferocious beast. The heroine clearly feels an inferiority to Blanche, but asserts Blanche's inferiority to her: 'Miss Ingram was a mark beneath jealousy: she was too inferior to excite the feeling.'

Adrienne Rich points out that Bertha Mason is Jane's alter ego[9], and, certainly, her characteristics are significantly opposite to those of Jane. Mr Rochester was first allured by her tall, dark, majestic form and sensual beauty, but then found her 'coarse', stupid, violent, 'intemperate', 'unchaste' and the giver of 'absurd, contradictory, exacting orders'.[10] The result is a 'monster' which Mr Rochester loathes and hides away. On two occasions, she attacks a man, setting fire to Mr Rochester's bed and stabbing her brother. As so often happens with magical thought, it seems that Bertha Mason is playing a dual role, being, in part, a character conjured up by the paternal aspect of Mr Rochester and, in part, created by the heroine's fears of her own will, powers and sexuality, and of what will happen to her if she expresses them within marriage to Rochester. This dual role arises from a single line of thought: when the heroine contemplates marriage to Rochester, she becomes haunted by the idea of this woman who expresses all her fears. As the third character in the primal triangle, the woman might appear a crazed, ferocious beast as a result of the heroine's fear of her and of what she means, and also as the result of her desire to cast her rival out. As the unacknowledged heroine, she is probably deformed by the heroine's fear of this self and of how her desired husband will view it; the captive madwoman may be her vision of the ultimate fate of this self in marriage.

The fifth move, which significantly cuts the fourth and sixth moves in half, begins with the heroine's recurring dreams about infants, some unhappy and some happy. These are rationalized as an omen of trouble, which arrives as bad news from Gateshead, but, at the level of fantasy, they are experienced as the heroine's return to thoughts of her childhood at Gateshead. In this move John and Mrs Reed die and the daughters, still presented as unpleasant, can no longer intimidate Jane. The heroine is concerned with how she feels about herself in relation to the Reeds. Now she is superior and is generous at Mrs Reed's deathbed, while Mrs Reed continues to be mean. Her hostility to Jane is explained as jealousy, Jane's mother having been a favourite with her uncle, and also as revenge for Jane's attack on her before going to Lowood. However, these explanations have little more force than rationalizations, as the magical concerns here are much more important than any imaginative attempt to transform the ogress with 'eye of flint' and 'inexorable soul'[11] into a woman whose motivation and point of view can be understood. Jane learns that her Uncle Eyre had wished to adopt her and make her the heir to his competency three years earlier, and Mrs Reed had told him that she died at Lowood. The intermittent news of Uncle Eyre's plans for the heroine express her estimation of her importance and independence.

The sixth move is at Thornfield once more: Mr Rochester is pretending to be marrying Blanche, but now events quickly move towards Jane's engagement to him. Mrs Fairfax expresses bewilderment: ' "He might almost be your father" ', she says, and Jane denies this, although this fact is central to her conflicts. However, she hates the way he treats her like 'a doll' and showers her with gifts. She longs for an 'independency' and writes to her Uncle John Eyre. It is this letter, significantly, which is to prevent her marriage to Rochester.

One night, just before the wedding, the heroine dreams that she is in a storm and longs to be with Mr Rochester, but there is a barrier between them. She is walking along an unknown road, trying to catch up with Rochester, but is burdened with a wailing child in her arms. He draws farther and farther away. Then she dreams that Thornfield Hall is a 'dreary ruin'; she is still burdened with the child and Mr Rochester is galloping away to a 'distant country'. She wakes to find the mysterious woman in her room: she has never actually seen her before and now the woman tears her wedding veil. The heroine's sense of her ability to marry Mr Rochester seems to be overcome by her feeling that she is only a child, and that there is a woman in Mr Rochester's life who makes this marriage impossible. Her future home is a ruin. Jane spends her last night before the wedding with Adèle, who seems 'the emblem of [her] past life.' Then the wedding is stopped because it is revealed that Mr Rochester is married to the mysterious woman, and on the acknowledgement of this the heroine refuses to have any relationship with him. The heroine takes her play of thought as far as the marriage, but her fears then prevent it. She has Mr Rochester identify the crazed, hidden-away creature as his wife, and this confirms both her fear of his dominance and her fear of incest.

Jane takes herself off into a deep exile, which is followed by an entry into a new and important move. With the Rivers cousins at Moor House, the heroine considers afresh her central preoccupations, making use of a new set of relatives distinctly parallel to the Reed cousins in the initial situation. The parent generation is absent, apart from the servant Hannah and the all-important Uncle Eyre, who dies, leaving Jane an independence which she shares with her cousins (this does not, however, solve her problem over independence). The move, as might be expected, shows a measure of reaction to the thoughts in the previous move; there is a change of mood in some ways similar to that in Horn's 'Goodmind' move, concentrated attention now being given to thoughts of service and sacrifice. It is significant that Morton School receives scant attention; we do not learn much about the pupils or Jane's experience of teaching them. The school seems to express a self-denying exile from that which the heroine really desires; it is felt as a negative experience, while she contemplates a life of virtue quite distinct from the life she has desired and condemned.

This seventh move takes the heroine a step forward in her struggle. The saintly cousin St John suggests that she should marry him in the name of service and sacrifice; and, as St John is a relative, and, to some extent, in a position parallel to that of Mr Rochester (as a masterful suitor), his proposal helps to resolve the heroine's conflicts over Mr Rochester. In her new mood the heroine experiments with the idea of marriage to a masterful relative, shadowed as it is by fear of incest and of the mastery, being undertaken in a spirit of self-denying virtue and renunciation.

St John is central to the heroine's magical purposes, and also highly developed by the novelist's art. His own service and sacrifice are established in his overcoming the temptation of Rosamund Oliver (a temptation not unlike that of Mr Rochester to Jane). He acquires 'a certain influence' over Jane which takes away her 'liberty of mind'; he wishes for her as a wife so that she can be his ' "sole helpmeet" ' whom he can ' "influence efficiently in life, and retain absolutely till death" '. Jane 'shuddered' as he said this.[12] Later, she imagines ' "the possibility of conceiving an inevitable, strange, torturing kind of love for him, because he is so talented, and there is often a certain heroic grandeur in his look, manner, and conversation. In that case, [her] lot would become unspeakably wretched." ' The magical and imaginative purposes in the creation of St John operate at quite different levels, and yet they are so much in harmony that it is difficult to distinguish between them. At the imaginative level, the novel explores what marriage to such a man, together with a life of service and sacrifice, might mean to Jane Eyre. At the magical level, the heroine is engaged in exorcism, exorcism of her fear of incest, and of her feeling that she should renounce the love she needs, and exorcism of the threat to her independence and selfhood which she senses to be inherent in the kind of marriage she desires. In St John she brings out these fears more sharply than she does in Mr Rochester, and her making him a dominating brother/father character, with whom marriage would be virtuous and a renunciation of love, gives her an opportunity to exorcise her sense of the evil in marriage to Mr Rochester.

The move ends just as the heroine is considering that she might, after all, be compelled to 'cease struggling with [St John] – to rush down the torrent of his will into the gulf of his existence, and there lose [her] own'. She suddenly hears her name being called by Rochester and responds 'I am coming!' She breaks from St John for, she says, 'It was *my* time to assume ascendancy. *My* powers were in play or in force.' The heroine has taken her play of thought almost to the point of surrender, and she then conjures up Mr Rochester's need of her and transfers herself to the last move. The transference to this new move has been made possible by the complete change of feeling brought about in the seventh move. Playing the idea of the parent husband combined with lovelessness and sacrifice as far as she can, in its full horror, she can now recoil. She knows she must have love and her ascendancy, and she has cleansed herself of guilt; she can now make renewed attempts to secure the parent husband who offers love. Among the devices she uses are her having St John speak the words describing how he will enslave her and herself reply that she will not marry without love, though she will still serve, while not his wife. Her proclamation of her ascendancy, moreover, has the power of magic words, further assisting the transference to the final move. The act of rejecting St John has probably also helped to cancel out the idea of incest in the love she seeks, while, at the same time, she is released from her felt obligation to renounce Mr Rochester and make a sacrifice of herself, when she has St John refuse the service she offers as a colleague rather than a wife. Her having offered the sacrifice and renunciation gives her a sense of her innocence in her final move. This is a complex network of feelings, and interpretation is difficult, but the crucial role of the seventh move in the fantasy as a whole is plain.

The new kind of relationship which the heroine creates in her last move at Ferndean reveals what more is needed for her to achieve a resolution. She arranges that Thornfield is burnt down by the wife who has haunted her, and that woman, expression of her fears about her desired husband, is now eliminated altogether, destroyed in her own blaze. Mr Rochester, meanwhile, has been blinded and crippled in trying to save her. Mr Rochester's Thornfield setting is exorcised and he is made a widower at Ferndean, no longer in a ménage haunted by a vision of the heroine destroyed and by women who appear to have a prior claim on him (Mrs Fairfax, Grace Poole, Bertha Mason and Blanche Ingram), while younger females (Jane and Adèle) have an ambiguous relationship to him as daughters and yet not daughters. His power and independence have also been lessened, and Jane says, ' "I love you better now, when I can really be useful to you, than I did in your state of proud independence, when you disdained every part but that of the giver and protector" '.[13] The financial independence bestowed by her Uncle Eyre, and the successful struggle with St John, have not been enough to give the heroine the marriage she desires and independence within it. The seventh move has prepared her, it seems, for violent action in her final move, where her fears of both dominance and incest are dealt with in relation to Mr Rochester himself. The home in which Mr Rochester is a father and the heroine only a child, or a crazed captive, is exorcised, and the parental characteristics which threatened the heroine's independence are destroyed: all that remains is the fatherly love, and, as the story now ends, this is the resolution to the heroine's conflicts.

Jane Eyre is a very interesting example of the multi-move fantasy structure. Conflict among the heroine's feelings propels the story through move after move, as the heroine repeatedly acts out these conflicts, seeking the victory of her wishes over opposing feelings. The story ends when, at last, she has achieved this victory. It is interesting to observe that she resorts to exorcism in her struggle to bring about a resolution: this is one of the many rituals resorted to in fantasy. Magical thought has to use magic to solve its problems; it has no recourse to the wisdom and judgement available to rational levels of thought.

As imaginative novelist, Charlotte Brontë has developed much of the content of the fantasy structure, and some of the moves have been considerably transformed by her directed and searching reflection on the nature of particular human problems. There is a penetrating exploration of which kinds of factors enslave and which factors make us free. The first and seventh moves (with Mrs Reed and Bessie, and with St John) are the most remarkable in this respect. Some of the content in the fantasy structure is also intensely realized in terms of outer reality, the second move, at Lowood School, being the finest in this regard. St John Rivers is developed as a striking and complicated individual: he is 'a good man' for whom the 'humanities and amenities of life [have] no attraction', a man who lives 'only to aspire – after what [is] good and great, certainly; but still he [will] never rest, nor approve of others resting round him'.[14] While St John plays an important role in the fantasy structure, the delineation of his character shows the skill and irony of the detached novelist.

However, much of the content of the fantasy structure has been left untransformed by the novelist; she has done little more than present it as if it were material having the same kind of reality as the details of life at Lowood School. In the moves at Thornfield, a simple indentification with Jane Eyre appears to be the key to all that is taking place, and the work emerges fully as a magical fantasy.[15]

In my next chapter I shall discuss two other ways in which fantasy and imaginative art can relate to each other in a single work of fiction. In Hans Christian Andersen's *The Ugly Duckling* they co-operate even more than they do in *Jane Eyre*, while in his *The Shadow* they operate quite separately from each other, without showing any of the harmony of purpose we find in *Jane Eyre*.

3

Two Stories by H. C. Andersen

In this chapter I shall discuss two contrasting ways in which fantasy may appear in literature, and the fact that the two stories used are by the same author[1] is an added interest in this regard. *The Ugly Duckling* has a complete fantasy structure incorporated in a design created by imaginative art, while *The Shadow* is also created by both fantasy and imaginative art, without there being any such co-operation between them. In *The Shadow* the purposes of fantasy and those of the imagination are quite separate and work against each other, creating discord. Fantasy cannot, of course, ever be aware of the imagination, but the imagination has, ideally, the ability to be aware of fantasy, this awareness giving it a measure of control over that level of thought.

The Ugly Duckling is a work of consummate artistry, meaningful from beginning to end both as a fantasy and as imaginative art, the fantasy structure being an integral part of the writer's total scheme. The fantasy gives the deeper and more limited view of the hero's experience, while the imaginative scheme extends our understanding of it, viewing it in the light of the realities of human behaviour. In such circumstances the extent of the writer's awareness as to the nature of the content of his story cannot be known and is not important. By contrast *The Shadow* is an example of a story containing material which needed examination on the part of the imaginative artist and did not receive it, perhaps because it was too close to the author. The result is a disturbing story, which has not attained popularity.

I
The Ugly Duckling

The Ugly Duckling may be appreciated as both an allegory and a magical story. The allegory and the fantasy share the same plot, and the author's larger contemplation of the hero's experiences, in the allegory, relates equally appropriately to the fantasy.

The allegory's most immediate concern seems to be with the fate of the child who is different and therefore unaccepted, while lacking the means of knowing his high quality until he is mature and has the chance of meeting his own kind. Communication is direct: absorption in the details of the narrative is our chief response, and there, through the author's choice of symbolism, especially that of 'the Ugly Duckling', we grasp the quality of the experience recounted. This symbolism also lends itself to the author's larger, imaginative exploration of the hero's circumstances. All the allegory's significance is readily accessible, for grasping it is largely a process of recognition; essentially, allegory assumes the audience already knows about the experience being symbolized.

Whatever our experience of the world, the experience of the 'Ugly Duckling' is known to us at the level of fantasy, where it is a state of mind, normally transitory. Our knowledge of it at this level must inform our contemplation of the allegory, which takes place, it seems, even as we also rehearse our experience magically.

The magical story has seven moves, the last containing a transformation scene. Five of these moves take place during the hero's exile, which extends between his initial and his final moves: this is due to the nature of the feelings with which he is contending. In this fantasy, the elements of the story are magical images rather than allegorical symbols, and they express the hero's solipsistic vision that he is different and therefore inferior and unlovable.

A study of the events of the story reveals how they express, at one and the same time, an allegory and a fantasy. I shall deal primarily with the fantasy at this point in my discussion, and afterwards consider how the author's imaginative purposes 'place' the hero's experience.

In the initial situation of his story, the hero is odd-man-out through being different, through not conforming in his personal appearance. Where behaviour is concerned, he does conform but everyone calls him ugly and is hostile towards him; he is surrounded by enemies. He therefore runs away into exile. First he meets some wild ducks, towards whom he is polite and graceful; they call him ugly, but say that this does not matter to them, provided he does not marry into their families. Next he meets two ganders who like his ugliness and suggest he joins them in their wooing of some geese, but they are then immediately killed in a hunt. The Duckling escapes death from one of the gun-dogs and thinks that this is because he is so ugly. Next he takes shelter in an old woman's hovel and is allowed to stay, as the old woman takes him for a fat duck which might lay eggs. Her much loved hen and cat jeer at him for not laying eggs and not purring, and for preferring swimming and diving instead. The Duckling goes into exile again and lives alone; all animals pass him by because he is so ugly. One evening he sees beautiful white birds which fill him with a great love and longing. He does not envy them their beauty and would be quite content if only the ducks in the duck-yard had tolerated him. Winter comes with its bitter cold, and the Duckling becomes exhausted through swimming to prevent his opening in the water from freezing up. A peasant rescues him from death but his family frightens the hero; he cannot do anything right in their house. Fortunately, their door is open and he gets away into his exile in the snow.

In the allegory these events express in a variety of ways the isolation of the child who does not fit in. Meanwhile, at the level of fantasy, the hero's five adventures in exile can be seen to be five moves, during which the hero thinks over his situation of outcast from five angles. These moves show a repetition of thoughts of the hero's being unacceptable because he is different. The wild ducks and the ganders respond to him in exactly opposite ways, but the ganders' acceptance of him is cancelled by death; moreover, he would have died with them, had he been one of them. In the move with the hen and the cat, the hero feels an outcast because he is different in nature and behaviour; in the move with the swans, he feels an outcast from beauty and splendour, and finally he feels an outcast even in the face of kindness, taking himself off into a long, wintry isolation.

To continue with the story, spring eventually comes, and the Duckling finds himself flying into a beautiful garden. There he sees the beautiful swans again and, seized once more with sadness, he decides to approach them to be killed for his ugliness. Better death from them than endure the rest of the world's enmity. But as he bows his head, waiting for death, he sees his reflection in the water. He is himself a swan. The other swans love him, people acclaim him as the most beautiful of all the swans; the world is full of friendship and warmth.

It is difficult to distinguish the magical thought from the imaginative purposes here, since they are in harmony and the hero does not use any obvious magical means to bring about the end of his story. In the allegory the events in the garden symbolize the hero's recognition of his identity and quality, when, at last, he has the opportunity to do so; while, in the fantasy, the hero's mood changes and he therefore enters into a new move, where winter becomes spring and the scene a beautiful garden, there to experience a transformation scene. The transformation scene is – as always – brought about largely by the change in the hero's feelings: his new mood enables him to see himself differently, and seeing himself differently reinforces his new mood, this bringing his story to an end.

There is a measure of recognition at the magical level, but it is not the result of a rational perception of a reality in terms of the perceived outer world, as it is in the allegory. It is a healthy adjustment of images, brought about by an adjustment of feelings. The hero dispels a grotesque self-image, created by negative feelings about himself, and substitutes an undistorted self-image, created by positive feelings about himself (which may be assisted by the magical powers of wish- or reassurance-fulfilment). As is also apparent in *Beauty and the Beast*, *The Weddynge of Sir Gawen and Dame Ragnell* and *Sir Gawain and the Green Knight*, the transformation scene creates images closer to those which reason might create – since they are no longer deformed by fear and other violent feelings – and of a kind which frees the hero so that he might be happier and more successful.

To turn now to the larger purposes of the allegory, Andersen develops certain aspects of the story, so that the hero's experiences, including the magical, can be seen from other points of view. He develops the animal reality, evoking the physical reality of being a cygnet, and bears in mind, in particular, the length of time which it takes a swan to reach maturity. This animal reality, and also the human reality which Andersen has before him in his imaginative vision, sometimes appear in ironic relationship with each other, as, for instance, in the mother duck's instructions to her brood that quarrelling over an eel's head, until it is lost to the cat, and an exaggerated consciousness of status and manners are both ways of the world. As we look back on the Duckling's loneliness and victimization, the animal reality tells us that cygnets are not ugly and that those so united against the Duckling (the ducks, the hen and the cat) are as different from each other as he is from them. The animal reality also tells us that, being the product of a swan's egg, the Duckling has always been a swan and, also, he truly cannot conform to other ways of life – he cannot become smaller, purr, or, as a male, lay eggs; there is no question of his compromising.

Even as the audience acutely feels the Duckling's sad story with him, the author's imaginative vision of the human scene conveys factors which lurk behind the attitudes shown towards the Duckling and behind the Duckling's own response. The conversations in the duck-yard and the hovel are so familiar that audiences must all recognize them instantly. In the hero's fantasy they may be taken at their face value, but put into the mouths of such characters living in such settings, their significance is sharpened. The hen and the cat are two rulers of the world dwelling in a hovel which is only standing up because it does not know which way to fall. They both possess an immense self-esteem which overrides all disadvantages, and this is why they win their argument with the Duckling. However, it is they who provocatively begin the argument: they clearly wish the Duckling to conform to their values and, at the same time, to be put in his place. Their self-esteem is fed by the agreement of others that living their way is best; and it is also fed by the defeat of others. They show an impatience with the Duckling's abilities and enjoyments which suggests the presence of that lurking envy which prevents people from rejoicing in joys they cannot share. By contrast with the hen and the cat, the Duckling can be seen to be suffering from lack of self-esteem. He is in agreement that he is of little worth, and if he is not on his own side he will not persuade anyone else to be. Thus, he cannot win: he could not win even in the home of the kindly peasants.

This dimension of the story 'places' the hero's experience, portraying it within the context of a greater comprehension of life, and one greater far than that of the hero's inner world. In order to 'place' the hero's experience, the author portrays the circumstances as he has observed them imaginatively; thus it is made possible for us to explore how such experiences as those of the hero come about. In this way the story is extended in content – especially when its outcome is known – from the story of an alienated hero who discovers his splendour to a much richer story which means for the audience whatever it is able to discern in the circumstances given.

In *The Ugly Duckling* we have both a complete imaginative story and a complete magical story. They share the same plot and co-operate, making an equally important contribution to the story's impact. The fantasy does so at the deeper, emotional level and the author's imaginative purposes do so through extending our understanding of the experience explored.

II

The Shadow

The interest of *The Shadow* for the present discussion is that this story exemplifies the problem of discrepancy of intention which sometimes arises in an individual writer's work. Traditional stories, well worn by their oral transmission among multitudes (who can only transmit what they understand), would not have any feature so confusing as discrepancy of intention. In the case of a story preserved in a book, there is little to prevent its appearance, beyond the writer's own vigilance.

The Shadow is told in the style of a writer distanced from his material and viewing it with some amusement. The tone is light and humorous, and there is a particularly delightful treatment of the behaviour of shadows. There can be no doubt that the author intended his tone to contrast sharply with the outcome of the events – the death of his hero, the scholar, at the hands of the shadow and the princess. He seems to be quite deliberately concerned with the power of a very low form of evil – a Peeping-Tom, parasitical form – to increase in dominance over good until the good is finally extinguished. The reason for this power on the part of such a form of evil is that people prefer it to goodness: there is more wealth and power to be obtained from knowledge which is damaging than there is from the scholar's learning. The contrast between the light tone and this theme is dramatic and effective. It appears to be designed to express the tragicomedy of a human wretchedness in which the knowledge of shameful deeds means power, and the knowledge of goodness, truth and beauty is extinguished by this other knowledge.

There can be no knowing how much a writer is consciously aware of, and nor is this of any great interest unless the total effect appears discordant and puzzling. This particular story simply does not add up. The first problem is that the Peeping-Tom activities, finding out the secrets of neighbours, are initiated by the scholar, who, instead of calling on his fascinating neighbour opposite, sets his shadow to spy on her. The second problem concerns this neighbour. She turns out to be Poetry, associated with beautiful literary themes by the scholar and claimed by the shadow as a source of all beauty and knowledge; nevertheless, only the shadow visits her and there is an unmistakable link between this visit and his subsequent Peeping-Tom activities to find out what everyone would like to know – his neighbour's secret evil deeds. The suggestion is that her secret deeds are evil too: why?

Perhaps Andersen means to show that the scholar is involved in the evil, but elsewhere in the story he is presented as a wholly good man. In fact, good and evil are split into separate units, the scholar being all good and the shadow all evil. Perhaps evil is all that the shadow is able to learn, even from Poetry. There appears to be double meaning in his description of the wisdom to be gained there, he himself selecting one meaning.

These answers are not wholly satisfactory. A Jungian might immediately jump to the conclusion that the shadow is the bad side of the scholar. One must never jump to conclusions when studying stories, but, here, there is evidence to suggest that the shadow is an aspect of the scholar, for the scholar makes his shadow enter Poetry's house by going through the appropriate movements himself. It is at the moment that he wishes to see inside Poetry's house that the splitting away of the shadow from the scholar takes place. Combining these factors with the subsequent Peeping-Tom activity of the shadow and the sinister suggestions surrounding the woman spied upon, there seems to be an underlying theme of spying to discover secrets about women, these being a source of power. All these matters are seen as evil. It is only one's evil self which engages in such dealings and these lead to more shameful evils, by means of which one's evil self will become stronger than one's good self and eventually destroy it. The shadow gains the princess and ultimate power primarily through his knowledge gained by peeping in at the palace windows. The princess's sharp sight, seen as a disease, has her choose the shadow as the wisest of men, while the scholar she accepts as wise but insubstantial, less than a man. However, when the wedding is announced, the scholar seeks to overpower his shadow and stop the marriage by divulging the truth. The final vision of his extinction and the shadow's triumph seems to be dominated by the thought that marriage can only take place when one's good self is annihilated, and thus no longer there to prevent it. And the princess herself is seen as deciding on this annihilation.

Some details in the text go a little way to define the evil. Poetry and the Princess are brought into a parallel relationship by the fact that the shadow spies on both of them and thus rises to power. Both spying activities lead to his becoming accepted as more substantial than the scholar, and to his gaining power through his items of knowledge. Describing his entry into Poetry's house, the shadow tells the eagerly questioning scholar that he saw everything which was to be seen; had the scholar come over, he would not have become a human being, but he, the shadow, became one (' "... jeg så alting, hvad der var at se! var De kommet derover, var De ikke blevet til menneske, men jeg blev det! ..." '). And, at the same time, the shadow learned to know his inmost nature, his inborn qualities, the affinity he had to poetry (' "... og tillige laerte jeg at kende min inderste natur, mit medfødte, det familieskab, jeg havde med Poesien" ').[2] The language is suggestive, and 'familieskab', which I have translated as 'affinity', is particularly interesting here. It means 'kinship' rather than 'relationship', and connotes a deep, formative, inner affinity, which could express equally well both Andersen's imaginative meaning and an underlying magical meaning; it probably expresses both. At the magical level, Poetry is a woman, not poetry, and it is his affinity to the woman that the shadow learns to know together with his natural, instinctive self. Whether or not thoughts of incest lurk among them, all these details in combination suggest that sexual knowledge is the evil knowledge acquired by the shadow; and the parallel relationship of the two female characters suggests that this is the case with the princess too. The hidden idea emerges fully into the narrative to shock us, when the scholar is executed so that his evil self can marry.

The presence of such a fantasy as this lurking beneath Andersen's imaginative purposes, and not woven into his design, would explain some of the story's discord. The lightness of his tone, at least, suggests that Andersen is unaware that the story has unhealthy implications. There does appear to be discrepancy of intention at the heart of the creative process in this story.

I shall now leave the study of magical fantasy temporarily, in order to discuss, through an examination of *The Lord of the Rings*, exactly how 'fantasy' contrived by the imagination and by intellectual ingenuity differs from it.

4

The Lord of the Rings

My purpose in this chapter is to clarify the difference between fantasy according to my definition and the work of the imagination, and also to distinguish between magic as created by fantasy and an intellectually contrived magical world. In *The Lord of the Rings*[1] it is possible to discern two separate creative activities, each creating what might be described as a structure, and neither of which is fantasy. One of these structures has been created at the verbal level of thought and the other at a deeply imaginative, less deliberate level of thought. The verbal structure is concerned with the action and with the organization of a magical world, while the deeper structure is a direct contemplation of the external world. As the story's magic has been imaginatively organized and the underlying structure, divided into cycles of thought, carries the deeper moral contemplation of the world, the work shows a very different arrangement from other works studied in this book.

Professor Randel Helms[2] and Dr Derek Brewer[3] discuss *The Lord of the Rings* as 'fantasy' (some of this being fantasy according to my definition) which is organized by imaginative purposes concerned with affairs in the external world and making use of symbols. Professor Helms sees the work as 'a political fantasy expressed in covert sexual symbols'[4]. He comments that the Orcs are symbols or representatives of a disruptive power inimical to established order, whose function is to rebel against and overthrow the status quo, like Blake's Orc, and there is sexual imagery in their presentation. However, Helms continues, while Blake's Orc is a symbolic picture of the return of the wrongfully repressed sexual impulses to the level of consciousness, and seen as beautiful, Tolkien's Orcs are disgusting and to be repressed in the Underworld of Mordor. Dr Brewer comments that, in a sense, the entire story is Frodo's dream of growing up and dying, and therefore our story too, by identification with Frodo. He sees Frodo as learning to escape the domination of parents and to establish relationships with his peers; Halflings are individuals emerging from childhood, and there is a profusion of parent figures, male and female, good and bad, which include Shelob, who is perhaps 'the Terrible Mother'. Dr Brewer also thinks that the Crack of Doom may be a 'repellent image of the engulfing sexuality that civilization must repudiate'.

Professor Helms and Dr Brewer mention subliminal matters and identification, but they are not distinguishing magical thought in *The Lord of the Rings*, for magical thought could not be concerned with political matters, human relationships or with what civilization must repudiate. Rightly, I believe, they perceive imaginative thought as creating the story. However, it is not their concern to make these distinctions, as it is mine. I wish to see more accurate definitions of 'fantasy' than are currently in use, and to suggest the need to examine all the detail of a work in context to ascertain what kind of thought is knitting that detail together. In my own study, I examine the clearly repetitive patterns in the construction of the work, patterns of repetition which correspond with the work's six books and which I call the six cycles of thought; and then I make a separate examination of the nature of Tolkien's magical world. As the reader pursues the linear form of the adventure in the magical world, the six cycles of thought are engaged in the separate and significant activity of repeating each other's concerns. The six cycles will be the chief subject of this chapter, but there will be a little further exploration of Tolkien's magical world in Chapter Six.

When reading Book I, one is interested first in how the adventures within that book parallel each other. This is the kind of relationship which is most likely, as it occurs in the moves of traditional fantasy and also in *The Hobbit* (where adventure after adventure repeats the idea of breaking into enemy territory and taking something). Professor Randel Helms discusses how the adventures in Book 1 of *The Lord of the Rings* are steps in an initiation; he also shows how the adventures in Book II parallel those in Book I in detail.[5] This present study will begin by showing how the first two books parallel each other in their fundamental concerns, and it will then examine each of the remaining books in turn. The six cycles of thought become clearer as the later books are examined.

Both Books I and II begin with a festive gathering: these are Bilbo's party in Book I and the hospitality at Rivendell in Book II. The two events contrast in spirit, Bilbo giving his birthday party in an antisocial mood, while the hospitality at Rivendell is generous. The events immediately following the festivities have striking similarities. On each occasion, there is a moment of antagonism over the Ring of Power owing to Bilbo's desire for it, and this event is followed by discussions centring on the danger of this Ring. It is decided that the Ring must be renounced.

The heroes then embark on a perilous journey, pursued by the enemy (Black Riders in Book I and black crows in Book II) and their first major adventure is an encounter with hostile nature: in Book I, the Old Forest and Old Man Willow, and, in Book II, the Pass of Caradhras and the Watcher in the Water. In Book I Sam saves Frodo when he is being held down in the water by Old Man Willow's root, and, in Book II, Sam saves Frodo again when he is seized by the Watcher in the Water's tentacle and about to be dragged into the water. Such parallels in detail between the two Books are frequent, and they will only be mentioned here when they are particularly useful in bringing to light the six cycles of thought. While nature is a formidable and enigmatic power in both Books, only Book I contains a character equally powerful. There, the heroes are rescued by Tom Bombadil, who shows that the powers of both nature and the Ring can become innocuous if one is part of nature and free of any relationships involving the overpowering of others or of oneself. He reverses the action of Old Man Willow and the Ring, when he rescues Merry and Pippin and when he makes the Ring invisible. By contrast, Gandalf is defeated by the Pass of Caradhras in Book II.

The second adventure in each Book is an encounter with death: in Book I, this encounter is the experience with the Barrow-wight and, in Book II, it is the discovery of Balin's tomb in Moria. On each occasion the heroes are underground; there is a passing through sleep and darkness and then the revelation, in a mysterious dim light, of friends, or a friend, in death. In the first Book, it is an imitation death, while the actual death is imminent, and in the second Book, the death has taken place. Sam, Merry and Pippin are rescued from the Barrow-wight, but Balin cannot be rescued. In Book I the Barrow-Downs adventure is concerned with the overcoming of death and the consequent acquiring of the instruments of good powers (elvish swords) which give an increased resistance to death-threatening evil. The swords are chosen for the heroes from the barrow treasure by life-affirming Tom Bombadil. The mental picture of Frodo's three companions arranged in a barrow as are those laid in such a grave confirms the fundamental subject matter of the episode. In the second Book, the treatment of the theme of death is more sombre – as also is the treatment of nature. This Book shows the threatening forces more powerful and the friendly forces less successful against them. While Tom Bombadil plays decisive roles against hostile nature and against death in Book I, Gandalf is defeated on the Pass of Caradhras and appears to be killed in Moria.

The ensuing adventures in Book I show the heroes, particularly Frodo, growing in knowledge of the determination of the evil enemy to seize the Ring of Power. This determination reaches a crisis point at the end of the Book, as Frodo faces the enemy alone, by the side of a river. He has to summon up his reserves of courage and decision, but unknown to him, help is near. The outcome is that Frodo retains the

Ring. He then rests with the elves at Rivendell. In Book II the order of events is altered, the sojourn with the elves (at Lórien) coming earlier than the crisis. Otherwise, the pattern of events is the same as in Book I: the enemy onslaught culminates in Frodo's facing a foe alone by the side of a river. This time the foe is Boromir. Frodo has to summon up the courage and decision to retain the Ring, and then has to make an important choice, making it on the basis of a much deeper knowledge than he possessed at the end of Book I. In both Books, the elves' powers for good play a role in imparting power to Frodo; in the first Book they give him practical help at the time of his crisis, and, in the second, Elrond's council and the teaching of Galadriel at Lórien give Frodo a knowledge upon which he can act alone.

After the encounter with death, the adventures seem to be directly concerned with the peril created by the desire for power, and the heroic qualities which can avert this peril. Each Book ends with the onslaught of the enemy having reached a crisis point, Frodo separated from his allies and having to engage his mind in overcoming fear and making a decision. The difference between the end of Book I and the end of Book II lies in Frodo's ability in Book II to deal with the crisis, and make his decisions, alone.

Book III does not have the same concern with initiation as do Books I and II, but it parallels them in a fashion which clarifies further just which are the chief concerns of *The Lord of the Rings* as a whole. Book III begins with a *rite de passage* and a ceremony, but this is not a bithday party, as in Book I, or a celebration of Frodo's recovery and escape from the Ringwraiths, as in Book II: in Book III it is a death and a funeral. Boromir has destroyed the mutual support of the Fellowship through his lust for power, and has now fallen, trying to save two of the scattered company from the enemy. Nevertheless, when he tells Aragorn ' "I have failed' ", Aragorn kisses him, saying ' "No. . . . You have conquered. Few have gained such a victory. Be at peace!" ' Upon these words Boromir dies smiling and he is given the funeral of a hero. The patterns emerging draw one to consider this episode in relation to Bilbo's unsociable sociable occasion in Book I, in which, wearing and using the Ring of Power, he shows a combination of generosity and hostility towards his guests. The author seems to have an increasing concern with mutually supportive living, considering it as essential for survival and as vulnerable to the assault of those who would reject it or prefer to dominate others. Further to this, we can see in Aragorn's generosity towards Boromir an enlargening 'rightness' which is set off against Bilbo's ultimate meanness towards his guests, leaving him shrunken. In Book II, Elrond's feast contrasts with the moment when Frodo shows Bilbo the Ring and then sees him as 'a little wrinkled creature' whom he wishes to strike. Again one senses the author's vision that survival and greatness lie in mutually supportive living, while there is instant danger and diminishment in power-seeking.

To return to the events in Book III, the capture by the Uruk-hai of Merry and Pippin, and their pursuit by Aragorn, Legolas and Gimli, bring all five companions to the forest of Fanghorn, the abode of Treebeard. Equally dangerous journeys had brought the companions in Book I to the Old Forest, Old Man Willow and Tom Bombadil, and those in Book II to the Pass of Caradhras and the Watcher in the Water. By now the heroes have learnt that nature on Middle-earth has a mind of its own and can be a formidable opponent, while, when in a mutually supportive relationship with people, it can be friendly. Now the nature theme is further developed, and Treebeard and his forest dominate Book III with their vital help in the defeat of Saruman. All the former nature motifs are united in Treebeard and Fangorn. Most important of these is the goodness of Tom Bombadil and the elves, who are proof against the forces of evil because they live in a mutually supportive relationship with nature, not only in harmony with it but also as part of it. While nature is a dangerous force, often hostile and murderous, those people are most successful who understand its point of view and join forces with it. The force which terrifies the companions in Book I now becomes an ally against Saruman, who, as a power-seeker like Sauron, is a destroyer of nature.

It is significant that Gandalf now reappears in the Forest of Fangorn, having recuperated in the Forest of Lórien. He proceeds to Edoras and revives King Théoden from a spiritual death brought about by the evil Wormtongue, secret servant of Saruman. This episode, following on that of Fangorn, can be seen to parallel the Barrow-Downs episode, which follows upon that of the Old Forest; and the Moria episode, which follows upon those of Caradhras and the Watcher in the Water. The theme of death is developing, for this third episode significantly differs from the previous two, even as it significantly resembles them. In a room lit by a dim and unusual light, the companions see a potential comrade being destroyed by the evil Wormtongue. The power of Gandalf, which has overcome his own death brought about by evil, overcomes the threat of Wormtongue and revives Théoden. In a fashion reminiscent of Tom Bombadil's rescue of the hobbits, Gandalf takes Théoden out of the dark hall of death and makes a new man of him. The victory over death won by Gandalf and Théoden then combines with the forces of Treebeard to win a victory over evil.

A direct struggle with the power-seekers follows this encounter with death, as it does in the previous books, this time beginning with the battle at Helm's Deep. The battle is won, but a greater crisis is reached afterwards, when Pippin finds himself face to face with Sauron in the Palantír. Had Sauron not believed that Pippin was in the hands of Saruman and therefore about to be handed over to him, he would have obtained all the information he wanted from Pippin immediately and won his quest for the Ring. It is Gandalf who makes the quick decision needed that he and Pippin should fly to Minas Tirith. Thus Book III ends.

In Book IV the initial concern with social occasion and relationship appears as an encounter – at last – with Gollum, and it gives rise to the most significant and complex relationship in the story. It is Frodo's intelligence, pity and courage which enable this strange but vital relationship, based on the interests of both parties, to form. It is, of course, under constant threat from the lure of the Ring.

Gollum now becomes their guide and leads them across the Dead Marshes. This is a place of death, likely to be their grave at any moment and already the grave of innumerable men fallen in battle (the Marshes having swallowed up their graves). Looking in the water the companions can see the dead faces, which are ' "Only shapes to see. . . . not to touch" '.

This adventure is followed by the journey up to the Black Gate, over land destroyed by Sauron, where there is no life of any kind at all – a land 'more loathsome far' than 'the Mere of Dead Faces' where 'some haggard phantom of green spring would come'. Then, proceeding to the alternative route into Mordor, the companions arrive at the fertile country of Ithilien and here Sam lovingly cooks a meal for Frodo. The smoke attracts Faramir and his men. After carefully ascertaining who the hobbits are, Faramir gives them shelter, food and advice, and is later able to tell Gandalf Frodo's plan.

These episodes echo those of nature and death in the previous book, and once again with interesting differences. Threatening nature and death are compounded and then there follows a contrasting episode amid fertile nature, love, refreshment and a furthering of the plans of the allies. As in the other Books, the heroes encounter and effectively deal in some way with nature and death before encountering a particularly formidable onslaught of the enemy seeking the One Ring of Power, and eventually (in the case of one of them) having to make a difficult and courageous decision. In Book IV, Frodo and Sam face Cirith Ungol and Shelob, the two forces guarding their chosen entrance into Mordor, and it is Sam who has to make the decision as to what to do when Frodo appears to be dead. He does so, only to learn too late that he has been mistaken, for Frodo is still alive – and now in the hands of the enemy.

In Book V, the initial social occasion and relationship appear in the form of the arrival of Gandalf and Pippin in Minas Tirith – with not a moment to spare if the city and Gondor itself are to be saved – only to be greeted by the Steward Denethor in an inappropriate and inhospitable manner. Denethor ignores Gandalf and wishes only to hear from Pippin about his son Boromir's death. There is no teaming up and pooling of resources to defeat a common enemy. Denethor's behaviour is puzzling because one is in doubt as to whose side he is on, and the truth emerges only later that Denethor's ability to enter into mutually supportive relationships has been diminished by the power-seekers, and thus the opening of Book V echoes the opening of the previous books. In this case, Denethor has been ' "too great" ' to submit to Sauron, but direct contact with him has given him a knowledge of his power which has reduced him to despair.

The next episode is Aragorn's journey through the Paths of the Dead to call up the dead oathbreakers who had failed to help in Isildur's war against Sauron in their lifetime, 'for they had worshipped Sauron in the Dark Years'. The Dead answer the call and travel with the Grey Company to play a decisive role in the defeat of the enemy. This further development of the theme of death has a particular relationship with its counterpart in Book II, for, once again, the encounter with death is combined with an underground journey, cutting through a range of mountains, as an alternative route to a destination on an urgent and perilous mission. The death episode in Book V also has an interesting relationship with that of nature in Book III: there the forest of Fangorn, similarly previously feared, becomes an essential ally, and now the Dead play that role. And just as the theme of nature tends to dominate Book III, so the theme of death tends to dominate Book V. Significantly, it appears before the nature theme in this Book – just as it also does in the sinister Book IV – and it appears again later in the activities of Denethor.

Further to this, Denethor has a dynamic relationship with Théoden. As Professor Helms points out, their names are virtual anagrams of each other.[6] They may be seen, too, to relate to each other in a number of small ways: each has lost his heir; each has a hobbit vowing service to him; each has a child rescued by that hobbit. Most important, each gives Gandalf an unfriendly welcome because each is under the power of the enemy, a power which is bringing about his own death. These similarities do not arise simply because the author is thinking fundamentally about the similarities: they arise, it seems, because he is thinking of the differences between the two men. One of them eventually listens to Gandalf and opts for life and opposition to the enemy, while the other does not listen to him and, ceasing to oppose the enemy, arranges his own death.

It is Théoden, not Denethor, who saves Minas Tirith, and he succeeds in doing this through the help of the Wild Men of the Woods.

Men living according to the rhythms of nature play a smaller role in Book V than does Treebeard in Book III, but it is nonetheless a decisive role. Also joined with Théoden in saving the city is Aragorn who, like Théoden, has defied death (in the Paths of the Dead) in the pursuit of victory. Through the enlistment of the help of the dead men and the nature men comes another victory over the enemy, although again not a final one.

The direct conflict with the power-seekers outside Minas Tirith is followed by the making of another perilous decision, this time to distract Sauron's eye from the Ring-bearers by attacking the Black Gate. At the Black Gate, Gandalf makes the further decision that the struggle against Sauron must continue, even though it appears that Frodo has fallen into Sauron's hands and might be returned in exchange for the capitulation of the allies. Book V ends in the middle of the ensuing battle.

In Book VI the initial meeting and relationship is the reunion of Frodo and his loving servant Sam in Cirith Ungol. It takes place in circumstances of the greatest danger and it is marred by Frodo's temporary but shocking anger when he finds that Sam has the Ring. Every one of these initial meetings contrasts in some way the generosity of those not seeking power with the smallness of those affected, directly or indirectly, by its lure.

However, the relationship is quickly repaired and the heroes struggle over the Land of Shadow, a dark, moribund, increasingly waterless land, destroyed by Sauron's pursuit of power. Finally, at Mount Doom, Frodo cannot return the Ring to the fire to be unmade; he cannot now renounce it and he puts it on. Sauron sees him and sends the Nazgûl 'faster than the winds' to seize the Ring and destroy the hobbits. The hobbits' doom would have been upon them if Gollum had not been there. He bites the Ring off Frodo's finger and, dancing for joy, falls into the Crack of Doom. ' "The Quest would have been in vain, even at the bitter end," ' if Gollum had not achieved it through his own death. The climax of the quest dwells on the death blow that the lust for power can deal to the natural world, creating a land in which people too must die of hunger and thirst. And the quest itself could only be achieved through the death of the possessor of the Ring, he who had sought to wield its power; this role is assumed by Gollum, already destroyed by the lure of the Ring. The hobbits survive only because the Ring is destroyed. One of the attributes of the Ring of Power is death: life can only be assured when it has been unmade.

The affirmation of that life comes in the succeeding chapters. Aragorn, who has already proved himself king through his healing powers, is crowned; and Faramir and Eowyn marry, planning to live in Ithilien. When the hobbits return to the Shire they find a devastation there brought about by Saruman, and thus there is further conflict with the power-seekers. However, they have little difficulty now in destroying this last remnant of the power-seeking enemy, and restoring, with Galadriel's magic soil, the Shire's trees and fertility. The Book ends with Sam's decision to marry and to invest his future in the Shire, while Frodo decides to leave the Shire for ever in the company of the bearers of the Three Rings.

While the last Book has a slightly different pattern from that of the others, the same themes are present. These themes might be summarized as follows:

1. Human relationships; greatness and the power to survive lie in mutually supportive relationships involving generosity. These things are threatened by those who seek dominance.
2. Nature; people can only be successful if they live as part of the natural world; human domination destroys the mutually supportive relationships which are possible in a state of equality, and thus will destroy both nature and humankind.
3. Death; man has to establish a relationship with death, discovering the forces which affirm life and learning to resist those which may bring about untimely death.
4. Power. This principal theme of the book becomes prominent at this particular point of each cycle. Throughout the work, there is a consideration of the peril created by the desire for dominance and of the heroic qualities which can avert this peril.
5. Decision-making; man's freedom of choice and decision is a momentous and difficult matter, especially as man has to be able to make decisions alone and when separated from important allies.

Many of the episodes are sharply visual in their presentation. There also seems to be a dynamic relationship between the linked episodes in different cycles: each theme is developed in distinct and usually contrasting facets.

Clearly, the six cycles of thought are concerned with affairs in the external world, and therefore any magical fantasy in the story can be no more than incidental. There are, undoubtedly, fragments of fantasy in the story, but the absence of a fantasy structure, giving the necessary contextual evidence, prevents there being any useful discussion as to where they may be found and what they mean. Resorting to the method of asking questions about apparent anomalies, the Shelob episode is a striking weakness in the story, and not only because it depends for its effects on the reader's being afraid of spiders. The episode does not seem to be integral with the story's fundamental themes: Shelob does not 'fit in' even at the level of the action; she has nothing to do with Sauron and the Ring. Perhaps we have an intrusive fragment of fantasy here, but I see no evidence to support Dr Brewer's suggestion that Shelob may be 'the Terrible Mother', in spite of her intriguing name.

As one follows the story at the level of the action, participating in the adventures, one finds oneself engaged in moral and tactical decision-making, using reasoning powers similar to those employed in everyday life. At the end of Book II, Boromir argues cogently that if Frodo would lend him the Ring, he could defeat the hosts of Mordor, while Frodo's present plan to travel into Mordor with the Ring would be offering the enemy every chance of seizing it. However, Boromir's arguments are countered by Frodo's knowledge that anything done through the power of the Ring turns to evil, and the person effectively wielding it will become another Dark Lord in the place of the one he has overthrown. Frodo can already discern the lust for power in Boromir and must resist him. He makes the perilous but sound decision to leave secretly and travel alone with the Ring to the place where it can be destroyed. It is at this level of thought that the entire adventure is followed.

And, yet, the world of Tolkien's story appears, superficially, to be almost as magical and impossible as that of a fantasy. The Ring is invested with immense powers for evil, and many other objects in the story have supernatural powers. A great number of the characters, too, have powers and characteristics unknown on Earth. They may be dead, like the Black Riders, or people turned into trees, like Treebeard and his people. Some are fairy-tale characters, such as wizards, dwarfs, elves and monsters. As the reader makes his way into the world of the story, he wishes to know exactly how everything in it works: he wishes to know the laws by which the Ring's powers work, and the laws by which people can be detected and overpowered by Sauron and the Black Riders; he also desires to know the special powers and attributes of all the strange characters and magical objects in the story. He has to know these things because he follows the story at rational levels of thought, where he assesses situations, works out strategies and anticipates moves as does Jim Hawkins in *Treasure Island*, while the laws of the world of the story do not always approximate to those of the perceived external world, as do the laws of Jim Hawkins's world. A set of laws for this magical world, which are coherent according to our rational schemata, has to be manufactured by the author; and these are explained to the reader as Frodo himself learns them, in the course of his adventures and his discussions with the wise. This is not necessary in fantasy, for the magical world of a shared fantasy has to do with the reality of our inner world; we already know how it works. An example of Tolkien's magical laws is the one by which a character becomes invisible to the natural world and visible to the powers of evil as soon as he puts on the Ring: this magic makes sense to our rational minds because we know that the very same forces that bring us under the power of evil can cut us off from others and from our natural environment.

The coherence of Middle-earth is not only a coherence at the immediate level of the action; it is a deeper coherence. This is a world in which moral laws, like magical laws, have the force of physical laws[7]: Tom Bombadil can make the Ring invisible and when anyone puts on the Ring, he can be physically seen by the Dark Lord. Meanwhile, goodness and evil themselves are functionally wholly separated and clearly defined. Goodness in a character can not only be total, it is also the result of the presence of certain concrete qualities, defined at the level of the action and also by the underlying six cycles of thought. It is known why Tom Bombadil is good: it has to do with his close relationship with nature, his life-affirming power, and his total lack of desire to dominate. On Middle-earth, moreover, goodness is more powerful than evil and can annihilate it, as Tom Bombadil shows when he makes the Ring invisible and does not feel its lure.

Professor Helms has an interesting discussion of the internal laws of Tolkien's secondary world, and he shows how the action relates to them; he also points out numerous parallels in the action detail. For example, one of the laws is that 'All experience is the realization of proverbial truth', and it might be seen that two proverbs structure the two parallel plot lines of Pippin and Merry: ' "generous deed should not be checked by cold counsel" ' and ' "Where will wants not, a way opens" '.[8] Gandalf speaks the first of these proverbs and Eowyn the second, and these are the characters who convey each hobbit from Rohan to Gondor. Each hobbit vows his service to a ruler (Denethor and Théoden) on a generous impulse, and each receives cold counsel from his lord. But, through his will, each is present to save the child of his lord (Faramir and Eowyn) from death.

In conclusion, *The Lord of the Rings* contains two distinct structures reflecting two distinct concerns, which work together in harmony. One of these structures is at the verbal level, and it is the concern of this structure to create a coherent, intellectually contrived magical world and also the action of the story taking place within it. A system of laws operating this imagined world has been logically worked out. The other structure underlies the first, and takes the form of imaginative, perhaps not deliberately planned, cycles of thought, contemplating affairs in the external world. These cycles are expressed largely through vivid images and they link up with each other in the pursuit of particular themes. The themes create a vision of the nature of goodness, evil, heroism and the power to survive, which informs the story as a whole. Any magical fantasy is incidental.

There will be a little further discussion of the magical world of *The Lord of the Rings* in Chapter Six, where the work will be compared with *Sir Gawain and the Green Knight*. I shall now turn to Chaucer's *The Wife of Bath's Tale* in order to study the author's treatment of a traditional fantasy. This contrasts informatively with the treatment of fantasy to be found in *Sir Gawain and the Green Knight* and *Hamlet*.

5

The Wife of Bath's Tale

In his *Wife of Bath's Tale*[1] Chaucer takes a traditional fantasy and transforms it so entirely for his own imaginative purposes that, at the level of the narrative, its magical purposes disappear. Nevertheless, he relies for some of his effects on his audience's knowledge of details in traditional versions of the story, including some of its magical elements. This chapter will examine Chaucer's use of the tale, to explore how his purposes differ from those of the fantasy and how he has used some of its elements. No particular versions are known to be his sources, and the versions he knew may be – superficially – different from any that have survived, but surviving versions show that the magical material is common to all of them. My study lends support to the view that it is important to investigate possible sources of *The Wife of Bath's Tale*, while it also supports the view that Chaucer's unique purposes have played an important role in creating the Tale.

The tale which Chaucer uses for his Wife of Bath is the ancient tale of the Loathly Lady, which appears in many cultures and takes a variety of forms[2]. I shall consider the Irish versions, to which Chaucer, like Chrestien de Troyes, may have had access[3], and the extant English versions, John Gower's 'Tale of Florent' in his *Confessio Amantis*[4], which is contemporary with *The Canterbury Tales*, and two versions which belong to the following century, the romance *The Weddynge of Sir Gawen and Dame Ragnell*[5] and the fragmentary ballad *The Marriage of Sir Gawaine*.[6]

One Irish version of the tale is the Munster story of Lughaid Laeighe[7], which might be summarized as follows. Dáire has six sons, all called Lughaid because of a prophecy that a son of his called Lughaid would rule Ireland. A druid tells Dáire that the son who becomes king will be the one who catches the golden fawn that comes to the assembly. When the golden fawn comes and is pursued by the men of Ireland, the six sons are closest behind him and a magic mist separates them from the rest of the pursuers. At last, Lughaid Laeighe collars the 'laegh' or 'fawn', hence his name. A snow storm causes one of the sons to search for a house, and he finds a mansion with a blazing fire, great supplies of food and drink, silver dishes and bedsteads of white bronze. A fearsome 'cailleach' or hag is also there and she asks him what he craves for. He replies, 'A bed till morning' and she says he may have it if he shares her bed. The young man refuses and returns to his brothers, the hag calling after him that he has missed the chance of kingship. The other sons enter one by one, and the hag asks each what he has met with. One has met with a wild pigling and eaten it, another has been overtaken by sleep, a third has missed catching a fawn and a fourth has eaten what the others have discarded; they are given appropriate nicknames by the hag. The last says that he has met with a fawn and alone eaten it; she calls him 'laeigh-de', meaning 'of-the-fawn-because-of-it'. In lieu of food and drink this Lughaid agrees to sleep with the hag, and the old woman gets into a white-bronze bed, followed by the young man. Suddenly she changes into a beautiful woman and he makes love to her; then she tells him that she is 'kingship' and he will have Ireland's rule. (The two other versions of the story – one of them in the *Cóir Anmann*[8] – also include these last important details.) They feast on the finest food and drink. The next morning the mansion has disappeared and the sons return to the assembly to tell their adventure. The version of the tale told of Lughaid which appears in the *Dindshenchas of Carn Máil*[9] includes a fearful description of the hag ('Broader her row of teeth . . . than a board set with draughtsmen' and so forth) and also the sons' horror: sooner than look upon 'that obese, lustful horror', they choose to be buried alive, and they give themselves over to a death of shame. The hag says that one of them must sleep with her or she will devour them all. The story is also told of Níall Nóighíallach, one of the five sons of Eochaid, in the *Temair Breg*[10] and the prose version *Echtra mac Echach Muigmedóin*.[11] The sons are out hunting and send one brother to a well, where he finds it guarded by an old and hideous hag (whose hideousness is described in detail). As the price of a drink she demands a kiss and he leaves in terror. The brothers go to the well in turn, one of them daring to give the hag a hasty kiss, which she tells him has earned him only a short visit to Tara. At last, Níall responds to the hag's request with enthusiasm, and she becomes beautiful, telling him that he will be heir to Tara. In the prose version she says, 'O king of Tara, I am the sovereignty', using the same Irish word ('flaithius') for 'sovereignty' ('kingship') as is used in the versions of the Lughaid Laeighe story.

Ananda K. Coomaraswamy[12] has pointed out that there are a number of Oriental parallels to this story and that there is a decided connection between the Loathly Lady stories and the *Fiers Baiser* stories, where the hero transforms the dragon or snake into a beautiful woman.[13] Meanwhile, Arthur C. L. Brown[14] points out that 'the Hateful *Fée*' appears again in the *Perceval* of Chrestien de Troyes and other Grail romances. A contemplation of the Indian parallels helps to liberate thought as to the nature of the content of the European stories. Ananda K. Coomaraswamy recounts the story of the snake-like bride of Indra, from whose lips Indra drinks the water of life, and whom he then purifies, thus making her fair. The names of Indra's consort suggest the Earth goddess and as such, we are told, they express dominion – not the dominion of the ruler himself, but the power, glory and fortune with which he operates. Ananda K. Coomaraswamy also tells us of the Indian goddess of fortune, Sri-Laksmi, who is, likewise, the goddess of all beauty, nourishment, kingship and dominion; she appears in her form of beauty only to those who deserve her. Her transformations reflect the fundamental polarity of good and bad fortune, and the changeability and fickleness of luck. Her 'Sri' manifestation (spendour) is the personification of the right to rule, the spirit of sovereignty, which can bestow the lordship on the successful hero. Ananda K. Coomaraswamy sees in these legends the notion that a king is espoused to his kingdom, as also does Proinsias MacCana[15], who sees in the Irish versions the early idea of sacral kingship, the king's ritual marriage to the realm. Ananda K. Coomaraswamy believes that, in a sense, the woman gives up her power to her lover – a suggestion I wish to bear in mind when considering *The Wife of Bath's Tale*.

Certainly, these stories do appear to unite the ideas of marriage and the right to rule land, or the taking of a woman and the taking of territory and power; these are ancient ideas, based partly on property ownership, patriliny and the sacral nature of kingship. But it is not enough to explain the Loathly Lady as the barren and unkempt land without its destined ruler[16], or as an expression of the battles that have to be fought to win royal rule (which is the post-transformation explanation in the prose version of Níall Nóighíallach's adventure with the hag). These explanations do not sufficiently account for the horror in the story, although the latter explanation touches upon the clear fact that the hero has fears to overcome before he can become the lover of the woman who can bestow sovereignty upon him. At the level of fantasy – if this is a fantasy, and the transformation scene suggests that it is – the woman's ugliness would be an expression of the hero's feelings about her; he would have put her under a spell, since *his* feelings and thoughts would be the source of the magic. As fantasies, the Loathly Lady stories would have something of the power of a magical rite to exorcise these fears; such a rite appears in the story of Indra's marriage, where a threefold purification action removes the bride's scaly reptilian skins. A final point which should be made here is that in the Irish stories and the story of Indra the woman is associated with the giving of nourishment, water or the water of life.

To turn now to the English versions, I shall begin by giving an outline of one of them, the romance of *The Weddynge of Sir Gawen and Dame Ragnell*. This romance begins with an account of King Arthur's solitary hunt in a forest, where he kills a hart. A huge knight, Sir Gromer Somer Joure, appears and threatens to kill him for giving his lands to Gawain; however, he changes the punishment to a task, which is to discover the answer to the riddle 'What is it which women love best?' Arthur has a year in which to find the answer and at the end of that time he is to return to the forest, unarmed, with it. Death is the penalty for failing to fulfil the task and the task must be kept secret. Arthur, however, tells Gawain, who undertakes to help the king, and they travel for eleven months, filling books with answers to the riddle, until Gawain thinks that Arthur must be safe. In spite of this, the king seeks the answer once more in the forest and there meets the hideous Dame Ragnell, riding on a gay palfrey. She tells him that she knows the answer and will help, but if the answer she gives is the right one, her reward must be marriage with Gawain. The king says that he cannot bind Gawain to this, but, when asked, Gawain says that for Arthur's sake he would marry a fiend. Dame Ragnell tells Arthur that sovereignty over men is what women most desire, and the king takes this answer to Sir Gromer. Sir Gromer is enraged, crying that it is his sister Ragnell who has told Arthur and that he wishes to see her burn. Meanwhile, Ragnell insists on her marriage taking place at once and openly, with a big marriage feast, at which she wolfs her food in a manner which appals everyone. In bed she pleads for a kiss and Gawain courteously says, 'I wolle do more Then for to kysse, and God before!' Immediately, she becomes young and beautiful and asks the delighted Gawain whether he would rather have her fair by night or fair by day. After deliberation, Gawain gives her the choice, for he cannot come to a decision himself. The bride then declares that since she has been given the sovereignty and is 'worshyppyd', she will always be fair. She explains that she was transformed by her stepmother to be ugly until the best knight in England would marry her and give her the sovereignty. A night of love follows, and all is explained to the rejoicing court the next day. King Arthur and Sir Gromer, meanwhile, become reconciled.

Like this romance, the other English versions combine the Loathly Lady story with the story of the man whose life depends on the correct answering of a question. (*The Wife of Bath's Tale* also does so.) The question is always 'What do women most desire (or love)?' and 'sovereignty' over men (or their 'will', in the ballad version) is the answer. The incidents leading up to the asking of the question are different in each version. In Gower's version, where there is only one hero, Florent, the question is asked by the grandmother of the man whom the hero has killed, and its motive is vengeance: it will bring about the death of Florent without blame to anyone. Unless he can answer the question, he must die. The ballad, which is close to the romance, has a belligerent baron set the question, as an alternative to making Arthur engage in a fight, and no reason has survived in this incomplete text. In view of the general craziness of these English versions, the addition of the riddle having only increased the craziness, it seems insufficient merely to point out that the question seems a silly one for the questioners to ask in the circumstances: why should any of these particular questioners be concerned with making the hero find out what women most desire – and as an act of vengeance, too? The answer to the question is given by the Loathly Lady in all three versions, her price being marriage, and this answer has an amusing relationship to the apparent content of the Irish stories.

All three stories describe the ugliness of the Lady in horrific detail, as do the Irish stories. Gower's version also agrees with the Irish stories that the Lady is old, and the romance implies this in its transformation scene. In both the romance and ballad, the Lady is sister to the belligerent knight, who swears vengeance on her for giving away the answer, and, in Gower, there may be a cognate, hidden relationship between the menacing grandmother and the elderly Loathly Lady – and also the stepmother, who is given in all three versions as the reason why the Lady appears as she does. The three stories agree – while Chaucer's version differs significantly – over most of the events following the meeting with the Loathly Lady.

Looking at the detail of the romance summarized above, and dealing with it as the creation of magical thought, the link in idea between the taking of the woman and the taking of property appears to be present. If we understand Arthur and Gawain both to be the hero, there are thoughts of the theft of land by the hero from Sir Gromer Somer Joure at the beginning of the story and what the hero actually gains from him is his sister. The idea of the hero's having fears to overcome before he can embrace the woman is also present, and a stepmother is the cause of the enchantment. The enchantment is really caused by the hero and it may well be prompted by a stepmother: 'sister' and 'stepmother' are typical disguises used by magical fantasy, and it appears that the hero succeeds in dispelling associations with a powerful mother-figure which haunt his thoughts of the woman. This would be in tune with the Irish stories in so far as their hag is old, usually a giver and withholder of nourishment or water, and one with the power to reward or punish. The shame felt by the *Carn Máil* heroes on beholding the 'lustful horror' is a detail lending weight to such an interpretation.

It might be speculated that the Loathly Lady stories are magical fantasies concerned with the achievement of the crucial transition that men have to make before attaining adult status and marriage (their 'kingdom'): they have to cease to relate to women as mothers – dominant, nurturing and taboo – and become able to relate to them as sexual partners. At the magical level of thought, people tend to be seen according to the primal experience of infancy, with a consequent confusion which can only be dealt with at this same level of thought. The vision of the powerful, maternal woman might be conjured up involuntarily or as the result of wishes. In either case, the enchantment is probably brought about by the hero's seeing his marriage partner in terms of his mother, this making her older, and also by his attendant fears of incest and of the dominant woman herself – which make her ugly. Where fear of incest is concerned, it is likely that ugliness is one of the defences fantasy sets up against finding someone attractive: when a hero is thinking of a woman who is taboo, he may see her as ugly because he is afraid of finding her beautiful. The Loathly Lady story may be a magical rite through which the hero dispels this fear, by taking the woman as a sexual partner in the face of his horror and within a set of enabling circumstances created by the story (such as the disguises, the Lady's command or pleading, or Sir Gawain's service to King Arthur). When the hero has taken the woman in deed or promise, she becomes fair and declares his transition: in the Irish versions she declares him a king and, in the English versions, she declares that she will always be fair. Her transformation to beauty is a result of his change of feeling, her beauty expressing his desire, and it is also a recognition that she is not what she seemed or who he thought. Furthermore, her transformation from age to youth may be exorcising her maternal aspect. Whatever the meaning, her declaration would act as magic words, giving power to the hero's greatest wishes against his fears – which might return, bringing with them the repulsive vision of the woman.

The combination of this fantasy with the riddle about women, which the hero has to answer to save his life, is harmonious. 'Sovereignty' as the answer to the riddle, and the gift the woman wishes to receive, seems a separate concern from the hero's fears, but the link might be his sense of the woman's power, which is present in the Irish stories too and might arise from her mother aspect. In the romance, Dame Ragnell takes charge of events from Sir Gromer, giving away the secret, and in Gower's version the grandmother is in charge of events from the beginning. The hero's sense of the woman's power is one of the elements of the fantasy which the Wife of Bath uses to further her own conscious convictions (not fantasies) about women; and the giving away of the secret, together with the transformation of the bride into a young and beautiful woman upon her husband's giving her the choice, are presented by the Wife as aspects of that power. However, even as she eclipses the purposes of the fantasy with her own purposes, turning a 'hero' fantasy into a 'heroine' imaginative tale, and an *exemplum* of her argument that women should have the sovereignty over men, Chaucer is sharing a joke with *his* audience, using its knowledge of the traditional tale. These matters I shall discuss in my examination of the Wife's Tale.

In the traditional versions of the story, the teller of the story is, of course, hidden, for, as the faithful re-creator of a fantasy, in which the teller and listeners identify with the hero and engage in solipsistic experience, he has no detached purposes where the story is concerned. By contrast, in *The Wife of Bath's Tale*, there are two known tellers of the tale: the detached author, with his own purposes, and his created character, the Wife of Bath, on whom he bestows separate purposes in order to fulfil his own. The author is not concerned with re-creating the tale faithfully; he is engaged in creating the Wife of Bath and is using the tale for these special fictional ends. Thus, far from idly identifying with a protagonist and participating in a shared dream, Chaucer's audience has the dual exercise of grasping the individual qualities of a unique fictional character, from whom it remains detached, and of trying to grasp the intentions of the ironic author organizing the fiction. The author keeps his audience guessing, partly because of the depth of his reflection on human character and its eternal equivocation, but also because he is teasing: with immeasurable skill, he leaves us in doubt as to how much the Wife intends and how much she does not intend, and as to the exact nature of his own intentions.

There are, of course, two audiences: the pilgrims, who are attending only to the Wife, and the audience external to the narrative, attending both to the Wife and to Chaucer. I shall use 'the Wife's audience' to refer to those attending to her, whether they be pilgrims or her wider audience, and 'Chaucer's audience' when I have to separate off those attending to his particular purposes, beyond the purposes bestowed upon his character.

Chaucer's audience has already come to know the Wife of Bath in her Prologue and, as her succeeding Tale proceeds, it realizes that the Prologue and Tale have a dynamic relationship with each other. Being aware of the peculiar interests and thinking of the narrator, this audience is concerned with these and with reflecting on her character much more than with hearing what happens to the knight and the Loathly Lady. Nevertheless, this audience's interest in the Wife centres on her treatment of the well-known story.

From the outset of her Tale, it is apparent that the Wife is engaged in a series of reversals, transferring power from men to women – an activity within her marriages which she has already recounted in her Prologue. She puts the Friar in his place, following an incident at the end of her Prologue, by using the fairy setting of her story as a chance to imply that friars rid the world of the traditional fairy rapists only to take their place. She then recounts that a knight of King Arthur's court rapes a maiden, for which he is condemned to be beheaded, until the queen and her ladies persuade the king to place the power of life and death over the knight into their hands. The Wife's shadowy King Arthur now recedes wholly into the background, leaving the court as one made up of a queen and her ladies rather than of the knights of the Round Table. Having obtained total power over the knight, the queen sets the question of the traditional story, and the man who has discounted a woman's wishes in order to satisfy his own can only save his life by turning his attention to the wishes of women. Furthermore, the Tale's beginning with allusions to rape on the part of the supposedly celibate and the reputedly chivalrous establishes the Wife's interest in placing men in an unflattering light.

As the Wife proceeds with her Tale, she uses her audience's knowledge of her sources in order to emphasize her point. 'Sovereignty' is the answer to the riddle and, as the Wife's audience thinks privately of the right answer, the Wife herself produces a list of suggested answers which make up a sum of attributes associated with sovereignty – riches, honour, praise, attentiveness, enjoyment, rich array and wisdom being among them. The list is in amusing contrast to the Wife's list in her Prologue of the female qualities which she claims please men (sexual parts, beauty, other bodily features, pleasing behaviour and the ability to amuse). The Wife is engaged in the unified task of overturning what she sees to be the male view of women and replacing it with her own view. Dramatically, the assembled desires are also clues to the right answer. The riddle about women, which is linked to the enigma at the heart of the fantasy, is one the Wife enjoys solving in detail, presenting her audience finally with an answer which, she thinks, makes good sense.

Another element in her sources which the Wife makes use of is the Loathly Lady's action in giving away the secret, and she presents this as an aspect of her power. Inability to keep a secret is among the qualities which the Wife claims for women, and she has already revealed in her Prologue that reticence is not a quality which she values herself. In particular, she tells us how she gave away to her friends shaming secrets about her husbands, and the digression in her Tale in which she gives her own, especially adapted, version of the story of Midas – the king's wife, rather than his barber, giving away the secret of his ass's ears – parallels this disclosure of a husband's shaming secrets. The Midas passage makes it clear that the Wife is engaged in another reversal here: in claiming indiscretion for women, she is concerned not so much with their weakness as with their power; she is asserting how men can be in the power of women. The Wife has herself emerged as largely immune from being in the power of others in this fashion, for she has happily given away her own private life in her Prologue; her immunity to the opinion of others is one of her sources of power. Meanwhile, in her Tale, the answer to a secret about women is being sought, and the knight, not being party to the secret, cannot 'give it away' to save his life, while a woman (the Loathly Lady) is able to give it away as good strategy. The Wife's women, as the possessors and disclosers of secrets (their own and those of others), are in a position of advantage and privilege and are a threat to men.

When the knight meets the Loathly Lady, she has an extraordinary power over him, a power even greater than we find in the other English versions. It seems that the Wife wishes to emphasize the Lady's magical power by associating her with fairies, for she tells her audience that the knight sees ladies dancing at the forest's edge and that they vanish, the knight then espying the old woman. There is no description of her hideousness; she is only old, ugly and wise, and the knight puts himself immediately into her power. He intends to use her answer, rather than any other, even before he knows what it is, before he is told how sound he will find it, and in spite of the fact that it, alone of all the answers he has been given, has an unknown price attached to it. He plights his troth that he will do the next thing she requires of him, while in all the other versions the hero knows what the Lady requires of him beforehand, and in Gower's version he offers all his other answers first. Why is he not more circumspect about the price? The Wife is arranging the story so as to emphasize the woman's power, at the same time expunging the horror felt by the hero, which is stressed at this point in every other version of the Loathly Lady fantasy.

However, when the Lady proclaims her side of the bargain before the court, the knight seems to have lost his sense of her power, and expresses his horror: she is no longer old and wise; she is just old and unmarriageable. The Wife must have a particular reason for this and I shall be taking up this point again.

The bedchamber scene is one of the Wife's most striking reversals. It bestows on the bride not only all the courtesy and generosity but also all the wisdom and learning. It is the knight who should have possessed these qualities, and Chaucer's contemporary, courtly, audience will have enjoyed this reversal. The Wife's knight is also the reverse of the traditional bridegrooms of the Lady, who, while perceiving her as horrific, make love to her either readily or with enthusiasm. The inclusion of the bride's discourse on the true origins of 'gentilesse' has been much disputed, since the uneducated, provincial Wife of Bath could not have had access to such a courtly concept; no more could she have known the authorities, Dante, Seneca and Boethius, brought forward to support the argument. What could Chaucer's purposes here be? The patient poverty which follows 'gentilesse' in the bride's discourses could have been hardly more possible to this extravagant, money-loving woman. While this suggests that the author is having some fun with his character, we can never be sure that he is not bestowing some of the teasing upon her; her manipulative playfulness has been amply revealed in her Prologue.[17]

However, the nature of the Wife's activity in telling her Tale is now becoming clearer. She is evidently identifying with the Loathly Lady, and altering her for this particular purpose. The original creature, whose fully described hideousness the Wife's audience will be remembering, is replaced by a woman who is old, ugly and low-born, declared unmarriageable but invested with magical powers to acquire a young husband. Chaucer is not only giving his Wife an *exemplum*, which she uses to support her argument that a submissive husband will be rewarded with a loving wife: he is also giving her an imaginative game; the tale lends itself to this ageing woman with a desire for fresh young men. The Wife is not replacing the 'hero' fantasy with another fantasy: her thought is not magical, because she uses her borrowed narrative elements to bring about her wishes within the context of the particular kind of relationship she desires, and at the same time she shows her audience what she means by this relationship. The Wife is concerned with human relationships, albeit in a somewhat egotistical way, and with argument and the manipulation of her audience – all of which concerns are the business of intellectual thought, not magical thought.

The Wife's identification with her Loathly Lady might help to explain the 'gentilesse' discourse. While the Wife bestows all the learning on the Lady, her audience will be remembering that in her fifth marriage it was her husband who had been – to her discomfort – the learned partner.[18] It is noteworthy, perhaps, rather than inexplicable, that the discourse is sound, not a parody: this enables Chaucer's audience to enjoy the ludicrous aspects of the Wife's vision the more, because we see it as she wishes it to be seen; it also adds to the amusement that only Chaucer, of the two narrators, can present the Wife's vision to us as she wishes it to be seen.

As the Wife's audience enjoys perceiving her wish-fulfilment vision, it must simultaneously make a comparison between her and the repulsive Lady of the fantasy: this comparison may be deepened by the recognition of the mother-figure in the Lady. When the Wife describes the knight's horror at going to bed with a woman who is old and low-born, her audience may bring to their response a memory of the horror of incest and of the dominant mother-figure, with her seemingly capricious wielding of her powers of reward and punishment, which may lie at the heart of the fantasy. And the Wife herself may prompt such uncomfortable thoughts, without recourse to the sources of her Tale.

Meanwhile, the Wife pursues her own distinct purpose, apparently oblivious to this particular effect of her Tale. Her knight has lost all sense of the power of her Lady, when faced with marrying her, and expresses only his horror in bed, because she wishes to present him as showing such attitudes to women in a position similar to her own and then to have her Lady use her powers to change them. The humour in the situation which she evokes of the older bride and the young husband is not only at her expense, for she reverses the much more familiar situation described in her Prologue, of the old husband and the young bride, and turns the tables on men in expecting them to be 'meeke, yonge and fressh abedde', while she does not feel equal obligations.

The Wife's purposes radically change the last part of the story. The magic – which, in the fantasy sources, originates in the thought of the hero (he is the enchanter) – is placed firmly in the hands of the Loathly bride. The stepmother is dispensed with, since the Wife's Loathly bride is not in the power of the knight's feelings about her. Moreover, the Wife's argumentative purposes dictate that the transformation does not take place until the bridegroom is thoroughly brought to heel; it does not take place until after he has given the choice to the bride, rather than before the choice is offered to him, as in the other versions. The choice itself is different, too: the bride places before the knight one which has many more vexing, practical implications than the one offered in the fantasy versions. She tells him that an old wife would not be tempted to be untrue, while a young, fair one would be; which would the knight have her be? The knight's dilemma is that he has to choose between two things which he would regard as essential in a wife – that she should attract him and that she should be faithful.[19] His inability to choose puts him further into his bride's power, giving the choice to her. Upon thus acquiring the sovereignty, the Wife's Lady transforms herself into a young, beautiful – and loving – wife, both to reward his submission and to delight her own wishes.

The Wife's purposes have eclipsed the magical purposes of her fantasy sources (purposes which would hardly appeal to her), but her very treatment of her sources – particularly her identification with her

Lady – serves to remind her audience of some of the magical content of the sources, as indeed does her personality. Apart from this joke which Chaucer shares with *his* audience, is there also a further enjoyment over the interpretation of 'sovereignty', a remembrance that, in the ancient stories, it is a notion the woman enshrines, and a power her husband wields? In the Irish stories, the woman who enshrines it gives it to her lover: does a memory of this work against the Wife's purposes in having the lover give it to the woman?

Whether or not the Irish stories were known to Chaucer, their promptings – and likewise the promptings of the English versions – are not entirely necessary. Stories with a fantasy structure are giving form to feelings and thoughts which are already familiar, and Ananda K. Coomaraswamy's work shows that the ideas behind the Loathly Lady story are common currency. There need not be any traditional link between the various versions of the story – although there probably is such a link between the 'sovereignty' versions. The fantasy that a woman is a kingdom may be present in any audience, alongside fantasies concerning the power of women, and these will inform its response to the Wife of Bath's Tale with all the magical force of fantasy. The response would be all the richer for the audience's being able to discern – rationally – the contrast between the Irish hero's vision and the Wife of Bath's.

In the next chapter, I shall study a fiction by another great medieval writer, which also makes use of a fantasy. In *Sir Gawain and the Green Knight*, the fantasy is faithfully and powerfully re-created, while there are also important imaginative purposes at work, operating separately but in harmony with the fantasy.

6

Sir Gawain and the Green Knight

This chapter will consider the medieval romance of *Sir Gawain and the Green Knight*[1], a great work of imaginative art in which the poet has, like Chaucer in his *The Wife of Bath's Tale*, made use of fantasy material, but in which he has not transformed the fantasy to the extent that it is entirely eclipsed. In *Sir Gawain and the Green Knight*, there is a complete fantasy structure underlying the entire work, which may or may not be the invention of the *Gawain*-poet. This fantasy is discussed in full in *Traditional Romance and Tale*[2], while here I shall undertake two further examinations of the work from fresh points of view. This will be useful, partly because of the doubt expressed by many critics that such a great work can contain a fantasy and also because it will provide further illumination as to the behaviour of fantasy. The first half of the chapter is devoted to a comparison between *Sir Gawain and the Green Knight* and another version of the same story, *The Grene Knight*: this comparison will reveal, in particular, that while apparent alterations take place during the transmission of a fantasy (whether it be in an oral or literary tradition), the altered surface details may be engaged in expressing the same fantasy, there being no real alteration at all. In the second half of the chapter, I compare *Sir Gawain and the Green Knight* and *The Lord of the Rings*, two works which have a dual concern with an adventure in a magical world and a moral vision of human dilemma, in order to explore how the two works differ in the expression of their dual concern.

I

Sir Gawain and the Green Knight and *The Grene Knight*

I shall begin the first discussion by giving a summary of *Sir Gawain and the Green Knight* to assist the reader, and also a brief account of the analysis of this romance which is made in *Traditional Romance and Tale*. These, of course, cannot really replace the original text and the original discussion, because of the importance of paying attention to every detail. The story of *Sir Gawain and the Green Knight*, which is dated about 1400 A.D., is as follows.

King Arthur holds court at Camelot at Christmas, and on New Year's Day he keeps his vow not to begin the feast before he has seen a marvel. As he waits, a huge knight comes riding into the hall, his clothing, horse, skin and hair all green in colour; he is also carrying a mighty axe and a holly bough. This knight challenges any of the company to a game: the knight accepting the challenge must deal him a blow with the axe and receive a blow from him in return a year later. The court is silent with amazement and the Green Knight laughs at them. Enraged, Arthur seizes the axe but his nephew, Gawain, who has been sitting next to Guinevere, asks for the adventure. He strikes off the green head with a single blow, and the Green Knight rises, picks up his head, reminds Gawain to keep his appointment at the Green Chapel a year later, and swiftly leaves the hall. The year passes, and after All Saints' Day Gawain sets out from Camelot in search of the Green Chapel. He searches in vain through a wintry wilderness full of perils until he comes upon a castle. It is Christmas Eve and the lord of the castle entertains him hospitably, while he is also welcomed by the beautiful lady of the castle and another lady who is ancient, hideous and unknown. When Gawain wishes to resume his quest on St John's Day, the host persuades him to remain three days longer, until New Year's morning, since the Green Chapel is near by. For the entertainment of Gawain, he suggests that they play a game: each evening host and guest will exchange whatever they have gained during the day. On the first day, the host hunts female deer in the forest, while his beautiful wife visits Gawain as he lies in bed and makes amorous advances, which Gawain resists; eventually, he courteously accepts a kiss from her. This he exchanges for the fair flesh of a doe, killed, beheaded and cut up by the lord. On the second day, the host hunts a dangerous boar, and the lady visits Gawain as he lies in bed, once more, this time telling him that he is strong enough to force her; Gawain accepts two kisses from her, these being exchanged for the boar's head. On the third day, the host hunts a wily fox, which is pursued with cries of 'thief', while the lady visits Gawain with naked breasts and back, persuading him to receive three kisses and also a green girdle, which he accepts because she tells him it will protect him during his ordeal the next day. Thinking of the Green Knight's axe, Gawain yields, promising to conceal the girdle from her lord. When the host hands him a fox's skin, he gives him the three kisses, but not the green girdle. The following day, he rides over the wintry hills into a wild valley, where he finds the Green Chapel, which turns out to be a hollow, grassy mound. He can hear the sound of an axe being sharpened and the Green Knight appears. Gawain flinches a little as the axe descends and the Green Knight witholds the axe, reproaching him. After another feint with the weapon, the Green Knight swings the axe a third time and only wounds Gawain slightly in the neck. Springing up to defend himself, Gawain discovers that the Green Knight is none other than his friendly host. The lord of the castle tells him that he is Bercilak de Hautdesert and that he himself planned the temptations at his castle; he knows all about Gawain's conduct. The slight wound punishes him for his lapse in perfect fidelity to his troth, his concealment of the green girdle. The whole scheme of the Green Knight has been devised by the hideous old woman at the castle, who is Morgan the Fay and Gawain's own aunt, her aim being to test the knights of the Round Table and to frighten Guinevere. The host invites Gawain to return to the castle, but Gawain is too ashamed to accept. Returning to Arthur's court, he wears the green girdle as a baldric in token of his fault, and the lords and ladies, who comfort him, wear similar green baldrics in honour of his loyalty.

Briefly, *Sir Gawain and the Green Knight* raises the kind of questions that fantasy always raises: the Green Knight and his extraordinary beheading game are fascinating and yet they make no sense to us if we consider them rationally, and, meanwhile, we wonder how Gawain could find the Green Knight again to keep his appointment without any directions whatsoever. Equally extraordinary is the fact that Gawain and his aunt spend Christmas together without Gawain's knowing who she is. And why is the fascinating Morgan the Fay a hideous old woman in this romance, especially as her brother, King Arthur, appears as a young man?

If we assume that Sir Gawain has invented this story and that he is thinking magically (his knightly thoughts being an imaginative overlay), the story emerges as a regular fantasy. It has two moves, one at Arthur's court (home to Gawain) and the other, as so often in fantasy, at a second castle. The characters in the first move are Gawain's uncle, King Arthur, the fair Guinevere, the hero and the Green Knight. In the second move, we find a lord as jovial as Arthur, his fair wife and a hideous, mysterious old woman, who turns out to be Gawain's aunt and a witch. Guinevere is also Gawain's aunt and also a fair wife. The repetition of character in successive moves, typical of magical fantasy, is apparent, and so also is the typical shape that fantasy takes. There is an initial move, followed by a perilous journey, this ending in the arrival at a longer place of adventure, in which the hero's feelings are acted out in full in the threefold bedroom, hunting and exchange scenes; at the end of this move a resolution is achieved. A study of the threefold sequence in the second move as the creation of the hero at the level of fantasy reveals a close relationship between the hunting scenes and the temptation scenes. The hero lies in bed, conjuring up the amorous lady and, meanwhile, he is out taking part in the hunt, where he sees the lord all-powerful over female deer and, at the same time, a slayer of timid animals. The thought is confused, as so often in fantasy, the lord being, to some extent, the hero and to some extent a father-figure, and the timid deer expressing both a vision of the lady and a vision of the hero himself. In the second sequence the hero thinks of a dangerous boar attacking the lord and being beheaded by him, and, at the same time, of the lady saying that he is strong enough to force her. In the third sequence he thinks of a wily, fearful fox being pursued and called a thief, while, in the bedchamber, he strips the lady in his thoughts so that her breasts and back are bare as she makes her advances. After he has accepted the three kisses and the green girdle from her, he sees the fox caught by the lord and reduced to a piece of skin.

Both games suggested by the Green Knight express the same thoughts, as the treatment of the hunted animals emphasizes. The approach to the Green Chapel parallels the conjuring up of the amorous lady, and the Green Knight's beheading game parallels the hunting scenes, in which timid, dangerous and thieving quarry are killed and dismembered by the lord of the castle. Every detail is an image engaged in expressing the hero's feelings; these feelings appear chiefly to be sexual desire accompanied by fear of punishment at the hands of a man with prior rights to the woman. The hunting scenes seem also to express the hero's sense that his feelings are harmful. Morgan the Fay is seen as the cause of it all, and she melds into the other women, Guinevere and the lady. Like the Loathly Lady, she appears as repulsive, and probably for the same reasons: her hideousness is the hero's defence against being attracted to her, and, moreover, her identity is repressed by the hero, so that he does not know who she is. Meanwhile, her enchantments are experienced in the form of a beautiful young woman, the deep disguise of displacement allowing these enchantments to be freely experienced.

An important feature is the transformation scene, in which the hero's vision of the Green Knight becomes his recognition that the Knight is the lord of the castle. It is possible that the recognition comes at the moment when the hero conjures up the image of the Green Chapel and the Green Knight side by side, and realizes that the Green Chapel, pictured as a grassy mound, is perfectly natural and that therefore a Green Knight would not be relevant to it. While a green chapel must be unnatural and probably expresses the hero's feeling that the object so described is taboo, the natural green mound is a picture of woman's sexual parts devoid of horror. The colour of the Green Knight, by contrast, suggests he cannot exist in nature, for green is a colour people cannot be.

While incomplete, this résumé of the discussion of *Sir Gawain and the Green Knight* in *Traditional Romance and Tale* is now sufficient for us to turn to *The Grene Knight*[3] for a comparison between the two stories.

Helaine Newstead comments in Severs' *A Manual of the Writings in Middle English*[4] that the tail-rhyme version appears to be a condensed version of *Sir Gawain and the Green Knight*, with none of the literary distinction that marks its model. Certainly, the arguments in favour of this verdict are strong and the study which I am about to make of the fantasy structure of *The Grene Knight* will show that the tail-rhyme writer has been faithful to the story as it appears in *Sir Gawain and the Green Knight*. But, whatever the origins of the tail-rhyme version, whether it be taken directly from *Sir Gawain and the Green Knight* or had some other source in literary tradition, a contemplation of both versions throws interesting light on the behaviour of fantasy in transmission, whether within an oral or literary tradition.

The Grene Knight opens at King Arthur's court, briefly describing the Christmas festivities, and then tells us that it is going to leave Arthur for Sir Bredbeddle, a man of great might and lord of great beauty. He loves his wife dearly as his life, but she is secretly in love with Sir Gawain, without ever having seen him, because he is strong in battle. She also has a mother, Agostes, a witch who can transform men so that they are as if they have been slain or wounded in battle.[5] She transforms Sir Bredbeddle for her daughter's sake (this transformation clearly making him unrecognizable, extraordinary and able to survive beheading, while greenness is restricted to his clothes and equipment); in this guise he is sent to Arthur's court. The reasons given for the mission are dual and distinct, the witch having her secret reasons and the knight giving others to the witch, on receiving his orders.

> shee said, "thou shalt to Arthurs hall;
> for there great aduentures shall befall
>   That euer saw King or Knight."
> all was for her daughters sake,
> that which she soe sadlye spake
>   to her sonne-in-law the Knight,
> because Sir Gawaine was bold and hardye,
> & thereto full of curtesye,
>   to bring him into her sight.
>
> the Knight said, "soe mote I thee,
> to Arthurs court will I mee hye
>   for to praise thee right,
> & to proue Gawaines point 3;
> & that be true that men tell me,
>   by Mary Most of might."[6]

When Sir Bredbeddle arrives at Arthur's court, the porter thinks him a 'Maruelous groome' and a sight such as he has never seen before. The Green Knight tells Arthur that he has come to prove 'poynts' that belong to manhood among his lords, and the king grants him his request, however he wishes to carry it out, whether through foot-fighting or through jousting for the love of fair ladies. The Green Knight presents his challenge that someone strike his head off, in exchange for a return blow at his head in a year's time. The beheading game is played, but not until after the Green Knight has dined with the company. Sir Kay asks for the adventure, saying that he will strike the Green Knight's neck in two and the head away from the body. He is told to be quiet and he then says that the company should make no boast of their blows; they are not aware of what they are doing – they are doing no good, but a great deal of evil. The adventure is granted to Sir Gawain. Outside the hall door, just before he leaves, the Green Knight puts his head back on again and tells Arthur that he will give Gawain a better blow in return. The tail-rhyme writer tells us that all this has been brought about by the witch's enchantment. Arthur becomes very ill and great mourning is made for him, while Guinevere weeps for his sake; the strength of his manhood cannot help and he is brought into great danger. Gawain comforts the king and queen and the company, saying that he has never been afraid in consequence of what he has done and is not frightened now; he does not know where the Green Chapel is but he will seek it. Meanwhile, returning home, the Green Knight does not answer his people's questions as to his 'doughtye deeds'; he knows full well that his wife loves Gawain. Sir Gawain leaves for the Green Chapel a year hence, in jewelled array, and, after journeying through a wilderness, he arrives at the fair castle of Sir Bredbeddle and asks for lodging for the night. Sir Bredbeddle takes him in and gets his wife to sup with him; she is described as doing so with her eyes upon Gawain. Sir Bredbeddle questions Gawain on the reasons for his journey, and the tail-rhyme writer tells us that had Sir Gawain known that he was the Green Knight, he would not have told him anything. Sir Bredbeddle tells Gawain the Chapel is nearby and that the master of it is a daring knight who works by witchcraft all the time, bringing about many a wonder; he suggests Gawain rests at his castle. They plight their troths to share whatever God sends them. In the morning Sir Bredbeddle goes out hunting and the old witch gets up, goes to her daughter and tells her that Gawain is staying in the castle all night long and she should not be afraid. She leads her to him, wakes the knight and tells him to take the body of this fair lady, who has loved him so dearly, in his arms.[7] She assures him that there is no man who can do him harm. Now they are both together, we are told, and the lady kisses Gawain three times; she says that her life will be in danger if she does not have his love. Sir Gawain looks[8] at the beautiful lady and says that her husband is a gentle knight and that it would be shameful if he injured one who has been kind to him. He thinks of his 'deede to doe' – the tryst with the Green Knight – and says he cannot rest or enjoy himself until it is over. The lady offers to help and gives him a white 'lace' which will save him from harm. Gawain thanks her and promises her to 'come againe'. Meanwhile, Sir Bredbeddle slays many a hind, wild boar and fox and, when it comes to the sharing, Gawain gives him the three kisses while concealing the lace. The next day, thanking and leaving the lady, Gawain goes to the Green Chapel, without knowing the way.

> euer more in his thought he had
> whether he shold worke as the Ladye bade,
>   that was soe curteous & sheene.[9]

Sir Bredbeddle, on his part, transforms himself and rides a different way. Gawain hears a horn blown upon a mountain and sees the Green Chapel under a hill covered with ivy (or yew trees); he also hears a sword being sharpened. There is one blow with the sword (just as there is only one visitation from the lady and one hunting expedition), and the Green Knight nicks Gawain's neck, blaming him for shrinking. Gawain then draws his sword and threatens to kill him.

> the Knight said withouten laine,
> "I wend I had Sir Gawaine slaine,
>   the gentlest Knight in this land;
> men told me of great renowne,
> of curtesie thou might haue woon the crowne
>   aboue both free & bound,
>
> "& alsoe of great gentrye;
> & now 3 points be put fro thee,
>   it is the Moe pittye:
> Sir Gawaine! thou wast not Leele
> when thou didst the lace conceale
>   that my wiffe gaue to thee!"[10]

Here the Green Knight suggests that the '3 points' are courtesy, nobility and loyalty, and that Gawain has forfeited them for not sharing the lace. After this, he adds that Gawain knew he had half the spoils from hunting. (Was Gawain expected to share the lace? – but a variety of such problems have arisen for those following the story at the imaginative level. How could this Green Knight have known about the lace, since his lady will hardly have told him? In the

Gawain-poet's version, the lady is described at the imaginative level as being in league with her lord, Sir Bercilak having sent her to test Gawain, and the sharing, moreover, is an exchange.) Sir Bredbeddle then says that if the lace had never been made, he would never have thought of slaying Gawain.

> "I wist it well my wiffe loued thee;
> thou wold doe me noe villanye,
>   but nicked her with nay;
> but wilt thou doe as I bidd thee,
> take me to Arthurs court with thee,
>   then were all to my pay."[11]

Sir Bredbeddle says that Gawain wished to do him no wrong and refused his wife firmly; he will be satisfied if Gawain takes him with him to Arthur's court. The knights make their peace and travel with light hearts to the court, spending the night at Hutton Castle on the way. The Court is delighted and Arthur grants Gawain's request that Knights of the Bath wear the lace till they have won their shoes or until a high-born lady takes it from a knight's neck because of his brave deeds.

The Grene Knight's similarity to *Sir Gawain and the Green Knight* and its many differences are equally intriguing. A detail such as the institution of the custom of wearing the lace at Arthur's court, altered as it is, suggests that the tail-rhyme writer had the *Gawain*-poet's work particularly in mind. One feels a similar conviction elsewhere in the romance: in the use of Christmas, in the inclusion of the reproach for Gawain's shrinking from the sword[12] (even though the sword – falchion – is different), and when the lace and the courtly qualities (courtesy and 'gentrye') reappear in spite of the fact that the popular tail-rhyme romances are not courtly literature.[13] Also significant is the reappearance of the three kisses and the three types of animal, even while the threefold temptation and hunting scenes do not reappear. Small differences in detail can be felt, at the imaginative level, to be unimportant, while one is struck by the similarities. At the same time, it is tempting to wonder whether intermediate versions were used as sources, perhaps alongside *Sir Gawain and the Green Knight*, since there are such a number of differences in superficial detail between the two romances. Some of these may originate in individual concerns on the part of the tail-rhyme writer, or the writer of an intermediate source: for example, when he places the fantasy in the external world, he chooses the 'west countrye', taking a Castle Flatting, in Delamere Forest, Cheshire, and also – confusingly – Carlisle, for Arthur's court, while a Hutton Castle is included, perhaps as the Green Knight's home. In *Sir Gawain and the Green*

Knight Arthur's court is at Camelot. A study of *The Grene Knight* at the level of fantasy will reveal a fantasy structure faithful to that appearing in *Sir Gawain and the Green Knight* (in spite of many apparent alterations) and with additional material superimposed upon it.

An immediately striking feature of *The Grene Knight* is the very different treatment of its Green Knight, lady and witch. The Green Knight is known to be Sir Bredbeddle throughout and sympathetically portrayed as a wronged husband. The lady, meanwhile, is not engaged in a scheme to test Gawain; she is truly in love with him. The witch is not much disguised in this version: we are told that she is the lady's mother and that her enchantments are identified with the lady's cause of love. In this less disguised version of the story, the moves are altered. The first move presents love, not testing, as the factor bringing about the adventure, the love being invested in a young woman, beautiful and forbidden, while the enchantments which fetch Gawain are created by the mother. In *Sir Gawain and the Green Knight*, where the feelings of temptation and fear are much greater, and hence the disguises greater, women are given no important role overtly in the first move – which takes place entirely at Arthur's court – and yet the repeat move patterns of the romance, together with the imagery, express their hidden presence. The tail-rhyme representation of the lady as in love with Gawain is not an alteration of *Sir Gawain and the Green Knight* at the level of fantasy, where the hero contemplates a secret love affair between himself and the lady. The love is all bestowed upon the lady, while the hero admits to none, partly because this is pleasing to the hero, partly because the hero has ambivalent feelings to express and partly because, at the level of fantasy, there is no distinction between a woman's deliberate lure and her passive attractiveness; the former might be assumed.

The Grene Knight's more explicit presentation of the fantasy contains some intriguing elaborations. The witch's enchantments are described as very destructive of men, rendering them as if they have come to grief in battle: this emphasizes a vision of woman inherent in her being presented as the cause of the beheading game. There is also an interesting elaboration in Sir Kay's intervention. At the level of fantasy, it presents alternative responses to the Green Knight's challenge, expressing first an aggressive acceptance, which is not allowed, and then a recoil and assertion that beheading the knight would be evil.[14] It should be noted that Gawain actually does what Kay first wishes to do – while his deed, unlike Kay's, is allowed by the king and company: he takes the axe to strike with eager will, and strikes the neck-bone in two, so that the blood bursts out from every vein and the head falls from the body. Arthur's illness is also an interesting addition – in spite of an ambuguity in the text as to whether the great peril which manhood may not surmount is that of King Arthur or Sir Gawain.[15] The illness is linked with the court's dismay over Gawain's danger, but, at the level of fantasy, it is logical that Arthur should be dangerously ill as a result of the beheading of the Green Knight. While the moves are altered in this version, the character repetition is identical with that found in the moves of *Sir Gawain and the Green Knight*. A fourth elaboration is Gawain's consideration of the lady's proposal to him as he rides to the Green Chapel: all the time, he is wondering whether he should do as the courteous and beautiful lady bids him. In *Sir Gawain and the Green Knight*, the hero's thoughts of a sexual approach to the lady are expressed only in the imagery of fantasy (the Green Chapel), not at the verbal level. Like many elaborations, this one helps to confirm the nature of the thought in the fantasy, where it is particularly obscure. There is a sureness in the tail-rhyme writer's grasp of the fantasy; his magical thought is fully engaged, as we might expect here. At the same time, it is tempting to wonder whether other versions of the fantasy have also been used as sources, since, if *Sir Gawain and the Green Knight* is the only source, we have to consider the tail-rhyme writer as one who combines the tendency to elaborate with the tendency to simplify. This is far from an impossible combination, but it might be that the elaborations – or the simplifications – are the work of intermediate writers.

The most notable of the simplifications in *The Grene Knight* are the lack of the threefold action sequence in the second move, and the absence of developed, detailed temptation and hunting scenes. These are combined with the lack of a moment of recognition, when the hero realizes the identity of the Green Knight (the audience knows his identity throughout, and the audience is, functionally, the hero), because he has realized that there is nothing to fear (there is little fear in this version). Combined, these omissions indicate a lack of development of the fantasy as a magical rite to bring about a solution to the hero's conflicts. *Sir Gawain and the Green Knight* is such a magical rite – and its lack of a transformation scene at the verbal level is quite unimportant; the audience experiences the recognition. In this great version, the colour green plays an important part in the ritual, but the tail-rhyme writer seems to have had some trouble with it. At first, we are told that only the knight's clothing is green, and the porter expresses wonder at this green clothing (' "all his vesture is greene" '[16]). The porter's amazement at the sight of the Green Knight is hardly explained by green clothing and we are not told in what other ways the knight is amazing. We are told that he has a green horse, but this is within the context of praise at the 'Iolly' (goodly) sight the Green Knight presents: horse, armour and weapons are all green and this suits him well. When, later, Sir Bredbeddle sets off for the Green Chapel, we are told he has changed himself into another guise, green as before.[17] The meaning is uncertain, but I suspect that the uncertainty is with the tail-rhyme writer rather than with his audience: he has not re-created the colour's role and, if he is working on the *Gawain*-poet's version, he may either not have grasped the more difficult magical thought or simply not be interested in it. His is a less profound, although otherwise quite accurate, re-creation of the fantasy.

The chief features of the transformation of Sir Bredbeddle are that he is unrecognizable (Gawain does not recognize him) and that he can survive beheading. These features are essential to the hero's vision in *Sir Gawain and the Green Knight*. The woman's enchantments result in there being a vision of a man to whom she belongs (the primal scene again) and this man is rendered changed and frightening. The woman's enchantments – which mean, of course, the hero's attraction to her – also lead to the beheading game, a game the man can survive. This beheading game seems not to be about death: the context suggests that it may be an image expressing castration. A variety of emotional experiences have created these images, and interpretation is difficult beyond the likelihood that they arise from the hero's feelings about the woman. The hero seems to see himself involved in an idea both dangerous and harmful, one leading to punishment and to the risk, as well as the test, of his manhood. While the enemy's special magical powers spring largely from the hero's fears, his survival and victory seem to have much to do with the hero's desire to restore rather than harm him. Further discussion will show how the tail-rhyme writer has brought to the fore the more wholesome elements here, the test of manhood and the love for the lord.

One of the most interesting features of *The Green Knight* is its treatment of the testing theme. The first lines I quote (in my otherwise unavoidably inadequate retelling of the story) declare the witch's purposes for enchanting the knight and sending him to Arthur's court as entirely those of love and as having nothing to do with testing the knights. It is the Green Knight who speaks of testing and, at the verbal level, there is confusion throughout as to what he is testing. He tells the witch that he will prove Gawain's 'points 3' and he tells Arthur that he has come to prove 'poynts' that belong to manhood among his lords. At the tryst, we learn that the '3 points' are courtesy, nobility and loyalty. These are, interestingly, on a different level from the proof of manhood as King Arthur understands it (he thinks the tests might be carried out by fighting), and they are also rather different from the qualities of Gawain which, we are told in the first verse I quote, attract the witch's daughter: bravery, toughness and courtesy. The Green Knight's treatment of Gawain after the second part of the beheading game is, at the imaginative level, puzzling altogether: he is both pleased and not pleased by Gawain's behaviour. Gawain's concealing the lace, instead of keeping his bargain of sharing his gains, leads to his forfeiting his knightly 'points 3'; but, as F. J. Furnivall points out in his edition of the romance[18], the three kisses and the lace could not be cut in half, and Gawain's giving the kisses while keeping the lace seems a fair sharing. The Green Knight seems unfair to Gawain, if we think in terms of *sharing*, but he is clearly not thinking of this bargain when he says that Gawain has done him 'noe villanye', saying 'nay' to his wife.

All these confused details help to place the testing theme. The more courtly elements in its expression (which might have been lifted from *Sir Gawain and the Green Knight*) are not always logically thought through so that they are constant throughout the story; they are also not integrated with the purposes of the fantasy. They appear as a random decoration. At the level of fantasy, it is the witch's purposes which bring about the beheading game – or, to take up the correct viewpoint, it is the hero's vision of the lady and her enchantments which does so. The witch is seen as sending the Green Knight to bring Gawain into her daughter's sight (or into her own – the text is ambiguous) because he is brave, tough and courteous, and we are independently told that the daughter loves Gawain because he is strong in battle. The Green Knight immediately responds that he will prove Gawain's 'points 3', and these 'points' might be assumed to be the three qualities admired by the witch's daughter (even though the witch does not mention either them or Gawain to the Green Knight). The Green Knight then tells Arthur that he has come to prove 'poynts' that belong to manhood, and the beheading game ensues, as if it is to be this test. At the level of fantasy, there are thoughts of a test – the test of the hero's manhood.

Another kind of test is also present. The hero loves the lady's husband and sees his amorous adventure as harmful to him. He thinks what a good man the husband is, even as he has the lady make love to him, this thought coming before his thoughts of the second part of the beheading game – his punishment. However, his secret adventure with the lady, like the concealment of the lace, is not seen as doing very much harm to her husband, as Sir Bredbeddle confirms in his scarcely cutting Gawain and in his magic words,

> "thou wold doe me noe villanye,
> but nicked her with nay".

This confirmation carries much more weight than the somewhat illogical and irrelevant announcement that Gawain has failed the test.

As the hero thinks of the lady being in love with him, he also thinks of the husband's responses, among these his watchfulness and judgement upon him: these are other reasons, apart from the hero's desire that his manhood be proved by the husband, for the Green Knight's stated purposes to the witch. The hero wins the approval of the Green Knight and the assurance of his friendship, and they go to Arthur's court together for a loving welcome. The testing at the level of fantasy is transformed by the *Gawain*-poet, while it is only decorated by the tail-rhyme writer, who has no coherent imaginative purposes.

A detail revealing the likelihood that *The Grene Knight* is a version of *Sir Gawain and the Green Knight* which has faithfully re-created the fantasy, while failing to give more than fragments of the imaginative themes, is Sir Bredbeddle's knowing about the concealment of the lace. It seems that the tail-rhyme writer has adopted this detail from the imaginative testing theme of *Sir Gawain and the Green Knight*, without adopting the entire theme within which it makes sense – the lady's role in the Green Knight's testing of Sir Gawain. The only scheme defining the lady's role in *The Grene Knight* is at the level of fantasy. The illogicality could simply have been ignored by the tail-rhyme writer, in the way that we do tend to fail to see such clashes between imaginative and magical purposes. Meanwhile, engaged as he is predominantly at the level of magical thought, and contemplating all his material from its limited viewpoint, the tail-rhyme writer would not be surprised at the Green Knight's knowing about the concealment of the lace; he has already bestowed the knowledge of the lady's secret love upon the Green Knight, and it seems that the hero believes within his magical vision that the Green Knight would possess all such knowledge.

Even as this study reveals magical thought out of touch with imaginative thought in *The Grene Knight*, it reveals the reverse in *Sir Gawain and the Green Knight*, where Morgan the Fay's given reasons for the beheading game – to test Arthur's knights and frighten Guinevere – can be seen to be amusingly different from the magical reasons. The fantasy lady-cum-witch's role has nothing to do with testing the hero; it is the Green Knight who does that. In *The Grene Knight* he does just that, even transforming himself for the task at the Green Chapel; the witch has nothing to do with this transformation. (We are told early in the romance that the witch has taught Sir Bredbeddle how to change his appearance.) That the Green Knight has his own personal, private business with the object of his wife's love is revealed in his not answering the questions of his people on his return home from the beheading at Arthur's court.

While the fantasy scheme in the two versions of the Green Knight story is fundamentally the same, the mood of the hero is different in each. The hero of *The Grene Knight* is light-hearted, as is made particularly clear in some detail not yet given: Sir Gawain's journey through the wilderness is rather pleasant: he sees many wonders, and birds near water as well as wild beasts. An examination of this version's magical purposes confirms the impression given by such surface detail. By contrast, *Sir Gawain and the Green Knight* is not only more weighty at the imaginative level, but also at the magical level, where the hero contends with deep conflicts, and struggles to resolve them by ritual and other magical means. The more sympathetic portrayal of the Green Knight in the tail-rhyme version arises largely from his being created by much less fear.

It does appear likely that the tail-rhyme writer has used *Sir Gawain and the Green Knight* as a source, and there is also a possibility that he has used intermediate or other versions as well. The fantasy itself might equally have been the invention of the *Gawain*-poet or of oral tradition, while the courtly material must have its origin in a literary tradition. Whatever the origins of *The Grene Knight*, a study of it is very informative, both about the process of fantasy transmission and about *Sir Gawain and the Green Knight*, going far to show the nature of the *Gawain*-poet's story material.

II

Sir Gawain and the Green Knight and *The Lord of the Rings*

It will be illuminating to consider *Sir Gawain and the Green Knight* in relation to *The Lord of the Rings*, since both works combine an adventure in a magical world with a moral contemplation of human conduct. Many critics insist that *Sir Gawain and the Green Knight* is essentially an artificial poem, a tightly constructed, 'consciously shaped' work of art: in what ways do the two works unite their concerns into 'consciously shaped' works of art?

It has been shown that *The Lord of the Rings* does so by a thorough interweaving of the author's two main concerns – the affairs of the magical secondary world of the story and the imaginative thought informing these affairs. These two concerns have each created a structure, the former the more deliberately created, while the latter may have taken form without the author's deliberate planning. The structures function in unison; they are never at odds. The former structure includes a logically worked out system of laws with which the action of the story interrelates: thus the magic is all under the imaginative control of the author. The latter structure takes the form of cycles resembling long, organized moves. Both structures carry the work's moral vision, but the imaginative cycles conduct the fuller moral exploration.

In *The Lord of the Rings* we have a magical world which relates meaningfully to our external world. A magical world must always relate meaningfully in some way to our experience – otherwise it would only be puzzling and boring – and it may either link up with the magical thinking of our inner world (in which case we know what it is all about even while it looks crazy to our rational minds), or it links up with our imaginative apprehension of how things are in the external world. In the latter case, the magical world has to be imaginatively constructed, since it cannot be one that is spontaneously shared, as in the former case. The laws by which it works have to be logically worked out if readers are to be able to participate in the story. The Ring of Power itself is magical: Frodo becomes invisible to the natural world as soon as he puts it on and visible to the powers of evil; a person of sufficient stature can use it to gain domination over the whole of Middle-earth. How can there be such a ring? But the fact is that we know all about this phenomenon. There are forces on Earth which can cut one off from the natural world and draw one under the influence of a lust to dominate and exploit the whole world. Certain kinds of people could succeed in realizing such an ambition.

Everything that takes place on Middle-earth makes good sense to the reasoning mind within the world of the story, impossible though it might be – in actual detail – on Earth. We are told that Sauron made the Ring, and he himself makes as much good sense as does the Ring; he is a familiar figure in our imaginative apprehension of the external world – the creator of a source of power greater than any other source. Temporarily, it has fallen into someone else's hands and this someone else has the chance to wield it effectively if he is big enough to do so; but provided that this someone does not wield it, Sauron can continue to build his power to some extent upon it. The Ring is about knowledge, knowledge of how to gain power over the world: knowledge created it and a great mind is required to wield it to full effect. That is why Sauron continues powerful while it still exists and is only destroyed when it is destroyed. The knowledge in anyone else's hands will weaken and threaten his power, but only seriously if the someone else can effectively use it. In actual detail, all this is impossible on Earth, for knowledge cannot be destroyed before the knower, but this is a smaller imaginative consideration than the felt need to renounce the perilous knowledge and unmake it to save Middle-earth from destruction.

Even as one looks closely at a detail in the magical world of *The Lord of the Rings*, one can see how coherent it is and also how it relates to the author's moral vision. Can we explain the Green Knight's beheading game in the way in which we can explain the lure of the Ring? Can we explain why Morgan the Fay should create the Green Knight and organize the beheading game, in as full and imaginatively as satisfactory a manner as we can explain the making and subsequent history of the Ring? The answer is that while the beheading game and the role of the fascinating witch catch the mind in some mysterious way, these things do not grip the reason and imagination which we bring to the world at large as having much meaning or importance: they appear pointless and trivial when compared with the issue of power in *The Lord of the Rings*.

The magical world of *Sir Gawain and the Green Knight* does not link up with our imaginative apprehension of how things are in the outer world. It is not, moreover, a world with a coherent system of laws enabling us to participate in the whole adventure with our intellectual skills of tactical manoeuvre, planning and investigation. While we do engage in tactical manoeuvre at the verbal level with the lady in the bedchamber scenes, we do not work out with the hero the best tactics for dealing with a magical knight according to laws which might be found to be governing his magic; we do not even investigate the whereabouts of the Green Chapel and plan the journey (there is, it appears, no problem here – even without an address – and the conduct of the journey is accorded comparatively little interest). The hero moves through his adventure with only the minimum of planning: apparently, things just happen to him and he responds in a manner befitting a knight of the Round Table. By contrast, Frodo finds out the laws governing Sauron's magical powers, and his tactic for dealing with him is the destruction of the Ring in the Crack of Doom. The route to the Crack of Doom is worked out in detail.

As in the case of *The Lord of the Rings*, *Sir Gawain and the Green Knight* has particular concerns at the verbal level and particular concerns pursued at a deeper level of the mind. In order to follow the former, in each work, one concentrates largely on the conversation of the characters, the details of the action and the descriptive passages. This is the easier level to study: one shares the characters' experiences, working out the next move with them in conversation and action, and feeling their world through the senses. It is at this level of the writing, at this most deliberate and conscious level, that the writer's chief, and perhaps his only conscious, purposes lie. In order to follow the deeper concern, one dwells on the work at levels of spontaneous emotional response, while also observing the pictures which the work creates in the mind, in the order in which they come. One looks for the patterns, for the repetitions, which lie below those created by verbal art. In *The Lord of the Rings*, six complete cycles underlying the action have been observed, repeating thoughts about human relationships, nature, death, power and decision-making. In *Sir Gawain and the Green Knight* the analysis in *Traditional Romance and Tale* has observed two cycles repeating thoughts of a dangerous game: this game involves injury, the extent of which is uncertain, to a formidable male adversary, which will be requited by a return injury. Further investigation of the cycles in both works involves following up the duplications of character and action which appear; in these duplications there will also be differences which are of great significance. In *The Lord of the Rings*, for example, we have Tom Bombadil and Treebeard from the nature theme and Théoden and Denethor from the death theme; and, where the action is concerned, we have the parallel gatherings or meetings, encounters with formidable nature and entries into tombs or tomblike places. In *Sir Gawain and the Green Knight* we have the king and queen of the first castle and the lord and lady – together with the old woman – of the second; the queen of the first castle and the old woman of the second are both aunts to Sir Gawain. Where the action is concerned, one should ask, for instance, whether the action at the first castle and that at the second (bedchamber and hunting scenes) are not parallel.

This inquiry is making quite obvious certain important differences between the two works under discussion. There is a much greater difficulty in discussing *Sir Gawain and the Green Knight* than there is in discussing *The Lord of the Rings*, once one approaches those aspects of the work beneath the surface features. In *The Lord of the Rings* the repeated subject matter, the character duplication and the more profound aspects of the action duplication can be discussed in such a way that the rational and imaginative mind immediately grasps the argument (whether it agrees with it or not). In *Sir Gawain and the Green Knight* this is not so: there, the repetitions are so indistinct that it is difficult to prove that they are there. Emphasis may or may not be a deliberate purpose of the cycles in *The Lord of the Rings*, but these cycles do have the effect of emphasis and this influences the reader's response to the whole work. In *Sir Gawain and the Green Knight* the reverse effect is apparent: the images and parallels are so obscure that they might be accused of being secretive, and secretiveness is a feature of material produced by magical thought. Thus the impression is deepened that the cycles of images in this work have been created at the level of fantasy.

Even while the cycles of thought underlying the romance may be the creations of fantasy, can it be said that they inform the author's imaginative themes of chivalry and the testing of Sir Gawain? Morgan the Fay's beheading game is, we are told by Sir Bercilak, intended to test the reputation of the Round Table, and it does indeed do so. It tests Sir Gawain's courage, honour, purity, courtesy and

Christian piety. The moral concern of *Sir Gawain and the Green Knight* is richly concentrated, the castles of King Arthur and Sir Bercilak showing not only the qualities particularly tested in Sir Gawain, but also the generosity, kindness and hospitality which are identified with the code of chivalry. The whole romance is warmed by the prevailing good feeling. The moral concern is at its most dramatic in the bedchamber scenes, where Sir Gawain has to maintain the highest standards of purity and honourable behaviour towards Sir Bercilak and his lady while also maintaining the highest standard of courtesy towards the lady. He achieves these with the utmost skill in the face of a formidable assault – although there is a small lapse at the end over the matter of courage, when he accepts the girdle, which he understands will protect him, and fails to return it to Sir Bercilak. The heart of Sir Gawain's testing, in the bedchamber and exchange scenes, is conveyed largely through conversation, and thus it has dramatic immediacy. However, the moral concern lacks the depth and dynamic force apparent in *The Lord of the Rings* because, at the level at which we follow Sir Gawain's testing, we do not know the full circumstances which have created the situation. The circumstances hint at being important, but they are elusive in meaning and are explained unsatisfactorily as being no more than the small-minded trickery of Morgan the Fay, who wishes to destroy a reputation and frighten a queen. Futhermore, goodness and evil are, at this level of comprehension, simply the qualities displayed by Sir Gawain, King Arthur and Sir Bercilak, and those qualities which Gawain succeeds in overcoming. Our concepts of these qualities are not nourished by the fuller exploration of their nature, meaning and importance which a consideration of them in relation to the whole situation might bring about.

As we concentrate on the work at the verbal level, we may not sense that there is anything unsatisfactory anywhere in it; very far from that, the richness of our experience at this level gives us the reverse impression. The poet's evocation of the chivalric world, the festivity of Christmas and the natural world has created a powerful work, and, meanwhile, the fantasy provides an adequate narrative framework for the testing. Also, audiences enjoying excellence at the imaginative level may have their attention diverted from features created for unrelated, magical purposes, especially when, as in this case, the unrelatedness is not particularly obtrusive. Moreover, it might well be felt that there is no need for thought clarifying and enriching the work's concepts of the goodness displayed by Arthur's knights and the evil threatening them: the goodness is already defined by the chivalric code, while the evil is conveyed powerfully and clearly enough as it is. However, this comparison of *Sir Gawain and the Green*

Knight and *The Lord of the Rings* has helped to bring out an important feature of the former work. As the romance is contemplated at both its verbal and deeper levels, it increasingly appears that, far from there being an interrelationship between these levels, there are really two works here, one created by the imagination and one created by fantasy. Each is created by quite different methods of thinking, and the only certain link between the two is that the latter supplies a plot outline upon which the former can be based, together with such accompanying feelings as temptation and fear. These kinds of link – together with the kind of questions the romance raises – indicate that the fantasy 'work' has an independent completeness, while the one created by the imagination is dependent and incomplete.

While there does appear to be a dichotomy between the concerns of the 'two works', the possibility of links needs a little further exploration. The chivalric themes are hardly present in the fantasy, but it would not be wholly true to say that the moral concern is confined to the imaginative level while the deeper levels of the work have nothing whatever to do with it. Concern which might be described as moral is expressed in the fantasy story, where Gawain's concern that the lord and lady should not be harmed wars with his desire for the lady. The hunting scenes, running parallel with the bedchamber scenes, best reveal that there are other feelings opposing Sir Gawain's desire besides fear of the axe, for they express his confused feelings during the dalliance in the bedchamber scenes. Among these confused feelings are the hero's concern that his thoughts about the lady are harmful and should therefore be terminated. These feelings are particularly apparent in the suffering of the does and the horrifying character of the boar (at which Gawain expresses horror at the verbal level). Such moral concern as this can hardly be described as moral *vision*, because it appears in the form of emotions among opposing emotions and is not considered in relation to a comprehensive vision of life. Nevertheless, there does appear to be some interaction between these feelings and the *Gawain*-poet's imaginative scheme; the feelings are evidently powerfully felt by the poet, and it is to be expected that there would be such harmony between the two levels of the work. The desire not to harm is more potent than any moral precept, and thus the hero's affective concern in the fantasy structure deepens the moral concern at the imaginative level; the latter would otherwise appeal to us less urgently.[19]

This investigation has revealed that the two distinct creative activities in *Sir Gawain and the Green Knight* are, unlike those of *The Lord of the Rings*, pursuing quite separate concerns. One is a creation or re-creation of a fantasy by magical thought, and the other is the imaginative creation of a chivalric story concerned with the testing of an Arthurian knight. The magical world is confined to the fantasy, and the moral concern mainly to the author's imaginative purposes. The harmony of feeling (*not* identity of feeling) existing between the two creative activities brings about a certain interaction in the case of the moral concern. However, the absence of any relationship between the methods of thought of the two creative activities means that the magical world cannot similarly interact with the chivalric world (being incomprehensible outside the fantasy structure). The dichotomy also limits the author's imaginative exploration of the issues in the chivalric story. It might finally be added that the richness of this famous romance seems to spring from the immense energy which the *Gawain*-poet has brought to both levels of thought and creation. The harmony of feeling has, of course, given the romance its over-all harmony.

I shall now turn to *Hamlet* to examine Shakespeare's re-creation of his fantasy sources. While we do not know what the *Gawain*-poet's sources were, we do know Shakespeare's likely sources, and it is therefore possible to explore the creative process at the level of fantasy side by side with the author's imaginative art. The relationship between the activities of fantasy and imaginative art in *Hamlet* appears to be of the same kind as that observed in *Sir Gawain and the Green Knight* and *Jane Eyre*: the development by the imagination of a fantasy plot, without there being the entire transformation of the fantasy which has been observed in *The Wife of Bath's Tale*. However, a study of Shakespeare's re-creation, rather than entire transformation, of his fantasy sources enables us to see how a great writer can operate at this level, making alterations to suit his purpose and yet remaining faithful to the fantasy.

7

Hamlet

Hamlet has been enjoyed by audiences as a rich and satisfying play, but the problems which it presents to those seeking to study it are almost as famous today as the play itself. The play is usually approached as one created by Shakespeare's imagination, as if it were a play similar in kind to *King Lear*, *Macbeth* and the other tragedies written when Shakespeare was at the height of his powers, and certainly the quality of its thought rewards exhaustive study. However, such exhaustive study does not answer the many questions which the play raises.

My investigation finds that Shakespeare's likely sources contain a fantasy structure, and that his contemplation of this fantasy has given rise, not, as in the case of Chaucer's *The Wife of Bath's Tale*, to its entire transformation into imaginative art, but to its faithful re-creation, this re-creation being accompanied by a parallel transformation of some of its content.

At the outset of my discussion of the play, it might seem that my results are to be similar to the findings of Freudian studies. Like the Freudians, I am concerned with fantasy, but my methods are quite different. My investigation, which examines the contextual evidence and does not introduce systems of ideas external to the text, finds support for some of the suggestions of Ernest Jones, but also produces different answers to important questions raised by the play.[1] Moreover, my analysis of the magical thought in Shakespeare's likely sources, which follows my examination of the play itself, is illuminating: a consideration of Shakespeare's play in the light of these versions deepens one's grasp of the reasons for such features in the play as Hamlet's uncrowned status, his delay and his treatment of Ophelia, and it throws light on the re-creation of fantasy material within a literary tradition.

The perusal of this chapter may prove interesting to those who wish to take another step towards solving the deep problems posed by *Hamlet*, but the account and analysis of the two texts which make up the sources are inevitably rather complicated.

I

Shakespeare's Play

Hamlet contains strange features, some of which defy an adequate rational explanation, and all of which link up together in a coherent fashion. I shall begin by surveying these features, relating those that are famous to others surprisingly little noticed.

The thirty-year-old prince of Denmark does not become king automatically upon his father's death, by hereditary right; and even while an English audience would expect him to become king instantly, and would therefore require explanations if it were following the play at a level of thought which is concerned with political realities, the matter is almost wholly ignored in the play. Instead, a cry goes up 'Laertes shall be king, Laertes king!'[2] Why should Laertes of all people be king? Such a cry is never raised for Hamlet, the prince.

Another vexed matter is that of Hamlet's delay in taking his revenge. It seems equally extraordinary that he suddenly becomes resolute when confronted with Laertes' avenging challenge, saying '... the readiness is all ... Let be.'[3]

Hamlet's treatment of Ophelia is another strange feature of the play. In the scene which Ophelia describes, he seems 'Mad' for her 'love' and, again, at her burial, he is her lover. But in the 'Get thee to a nunnery' scene, he speaks of her attractions as evil: they would make a monster of him and an object of 'calumny' of her. While marriage with the daughter of Polonius might be unsuitable for a prince, as Laertes tells Ophelia in their scene together before he goes abroad, it would not make a monster of Hamlet or cause Ophelia to be slandered.

In looking for the patterns of repetition in the play, one finds that there are some curious parallels among the characters and the incidents. There are also some interesting patterns in the times at which characters are on and off stage.

Laertes and Fortinbras parallel Hamlet in a remarkable number of respects, and play roles which we would expect the prince to play. Laertes, like the prince, becomes his father's avenger; and in the very scene before Claudius arranges that Hamlet should be spied upon by Rosencrantz and Guildenstern, Polonius arranges that Laertes should be spied upon while he is abroad. Again like Hamlet, Laertes shows a concern with the sexual life of a female relative: he speaks to Ophelia about protecting her 'chaste treasure' from Hamlet with a measure of urgency on the subject faintly resembling Hamlet's own violent words to his mother, accusing her of unfaithfulness and lust. Laertes plays a role which we would expect Hamlet to play when he rises in 'giant-like' 'rebellion' against Claudius, believing him to be the murderer of his father, and makes an apparent bid for the throne. Laertes also has a love for Ophelia which resembles that of a lover, and would be more fitting, as well as more welcome, in Hamlet. Before he goes abroad, he tells Ophelia:

> . . . do not sleep,
> But let me hear from you;

and at her burial he cries out:

> Hold off the earth awhile,
> Till I have caught her once more in mine arms . . .

In being an avenger who wastes no time, Laertes plays a role which does not surprise us where he is concerned, and which we would expect Hamlet to play.

Fortinbras corresponds to Hamlet in being subject to his uncle – 'old Norway' – and in being engaged in secret hostilities against the king of Denmark. Like Hamlet, he also deceives his uncle in the course of his hostilities, misleading him as to the nature of his activity. His 'levies . . . appeared' to his uncle 'To be a preparation 'gainst the Polack; But better looked into, he truly found It was against' Claudius.[4] Fortinbras plays roles which we would expect Hamlet to play in being active in his business of regaining property from the king of Denmark, and in concluding his hostilities by taking over the kingdom of Denmark.

It is interesting that Laertes and Hamlet rarely appear together in the play. When they do, they appear as opposite to each other. In their single appearance together early in the play, Laertes is granted leave to return abroad while Hamlet is bidden to remain at court. When they meet again, in the last part of the play, they do so as lovers of the same girl, opposing each other in her grave, and then, in the last scene, they fight each other to the death. Hamlet and Fortinbras also do not appear together, until the living Fortinbras appears beside the dead Hamlet and takes over the kingdom. The parts played by these three characters, combined with the pattern of their times on and off stage, suggest that, to some extent, they 'stand in' for each other.

Another curious feature of the play is the repetition of the spying motif. Polonius' arrangement that Laertes should be spied upon, and Claudius' arrangement that Hamlet should be spied upon, occur in adjacent scenes. Moreover, Hamlet has an interview alone with a woman on two occasions – once with Ophelia and once with his mother – and on each occasion he is spied upon by two king or father characters: by Claudius and Polonius on the first occasion and by

Polonius and King Hamlet on the second. The inclusion of the ghost in this duplication of the spying motif suggests that there is a link between the spying and the haunting.

Where the ghost is concerned, two reasons are given for his haunting. In the first scene, it is thought that he might be haunting because Fortinbras is mobilizing to regain the lands which his slain father lost to King Hamlet, and later he tells Hamlet that he is haunting because Claudius has murdered him and usurped his crown and queen. We are also told that the ghost is in armour: he is in the same armour as that which he wore when he killed 'ambitious' King Fortinbras of 'emulate pride' who had dared him to combat. The dual reason for the haunting brings the activity of Fortinbras into prominence and into a possibly significant relationship with the activity of Claudius. The wearing of the same armour links King Hamlet's overcoming of King Fortinbras with his present purposes: this is a ghost at war with those who would usurp his property.

The two women characters are linked through the duplication of Hamlet's interview alone with a woman. Not only is he spied upon by two father characters on each occasion, but he also uses each occasion to contemplate the woman's sexuality with disgust and bid her renounce it.

Polonius plays a role parallel in part to those of the kings Claudius and Hamlet. The three characters are linked together by their roles in the spying and haunting motifs, and Hamlet mistakes Polonius for Claudius in the scene in the queen's closet: '. . . is it the King? . . . I took thee for thy better . . .' Polonius becomes a murdered father, as King Hamlet is a murdered father, and his son avenges him. Ophelia confuses the murdered fathers when she sings that 'He is dead and gone' and has not gone to the grave with 'true-love' mourning. This will refer to both Polonius and King Hamlet, and the term 'true-love', linking as it does with the queen's 'true-love' ('How should I your true-love know From another one?') emphasizes that King Hamlet is also thought of.[5] Further details connecting the two fathers closely are the references to Julius Caesar. As the characters in the first scene of the play consider the ghost of King Hamlet, Horatio refers to the murder of Julius Caesar and the haunting of the 'sheeted dead' in connection with it. Later, Polonius tells Hamlet that he once 'did enact Julius Caesar . . . killed i' th' Capitol' by Brutus.[6]

These parallels do not appear to have an ironic purpose, as they might do if created by the imagination. Moreover, the characters and incidents are not brought into a dynamic relationship with each other in the expression of a many-sided imaginative vision of life. The nature of the repetitions suggests a dreamlike fragmentation of character and reiteration of theme.

There is a reiteration of the idea of secret hostilities against kings, usually in order to gain their property, and of the idea of revenge for such hostilities. There is also a reiteration of the watchful king or father, and of the woman relative whose sexuality interests a male relative in some way. The role of Polonius in these patterns suggests that kings and fathers are playing identical roles here; and the role of Claudius suggests that he is playing a dual part, as a king-father and as a murderous usurper.

The roles of Laertes and Fortinbras in relation to Hamlet's role suggest that they are 'repeat' characters of Hamlet, and that they play roles which the acknowledged hero, Hamlet, disowns or, for some reason, has chosen not to play. This impression is reinforced by some of the minor detail in the scene in the graveyard and at the play-within-the-play. The gravedigger tells us that Hamlet was born on the same day that King Hamlet overcame King Fortinbras, and that he himself began digging graves on that very day. Hamlet's birth is spoken of as if it were one with unsuccessful hostility against his father and one with death. During his commentary upon the action of his play-within-the-play, a drama which presents 'something like the murder of [his] father', Hamlet is 'as good as a chorus' and tells us that the play's murderer is 'nephew to the king', not brother. Such extraordinary information, imparted in such an inconsequential manner, might well be fantasy material, and, as such, extremely revealing as to the nature of the hero's preoccupations. An exploration of the drama as the invention of Hamlet himself might show how its strange features link up to express a coherent fantasy.

The hero is thinking of ambitious hostility against a king-father in a variety of ways, and also about how this hostility must be avenged. The king-father is seen as both murdered and as at war against the aggressor; and, during the course of the play, the aggressor is seen as both destroyed (King Fortinbras) and as successful, awaiting punishment. The aggressor is also seen as finally victorious, but it is essential to observe here that Prince Fortinbras has been opposed to the usurping king, Claudius.

The events in such a drama as this should not be seen as taking place in the same fictional sense in which we see Israel Hands' death or the Wife of Bath's marriages as taking place. They take place in the sense that the hero of the drama is thinking of their doing so, and the hero's thoughts are of such an ambiguous nature that there can be alternative events taking place in the same drama. While this is so, there is a central progression of thought, with a particular focus, which will now be examined through an attempt to unravel the role of the acknowledged hero, Hamlet.

From the outset of the play, Hamlet is a haunted man, haunted by a murdered father and by fathers watching him. Laertes' situation, as a son spied upon by his father, leads one to look more closely at Hamlet's parallel situation. Polonius arranges for Laertes to be spied upon so as to know his behaviour, and this hints that the spying of the ghost, and that of Claudius and Polonius, may also have the prime purpose of keeping a watch on Hamlet's behaviour. This purpose by no means conflicts with the ghost's stated purpose to incite Hamlet to revenge or with Claudius' and Polonius' purpose to observe Hamlet's feelings for Ophelia: the patterns of repetition suggest that the hero is haunted by the feeling that he is being watched by father characters where his hostility and his feelings about women relatives are concerned.

The hero bestows upon his acknowledged self, Hamlet, certain of his feelings only. Hamlet is the avenger of his father and is not concerned with usurping his position. He refers on only two brief occasions to his 'hopes' and to his lack of 'advancement'.[7] It would appear that the hero disowns the wish to be king, and the reason for this can be seen in the character who does become king: Claudius is an incestuous usurper who has murdered the king. The role of Fortinbras makes it clear that there is also another reason for Hamlet's lack of concern with his uncrowned status. Claudius must be dethroned and replaced, and it is Fortinbras who replaces him: the hero evidently has more important business on hand for Hamlet to deal with.

Hamlet is the avenger of his father, who cannot act. Claudius is the usurper against whom we expect him to act, and both Fortinbras and Laertes do act against him in different ways. Where Laertes' revenge is concerned, it is interesting to note that he makes a false start in believing that Claudius is the culprit and then challenges Hamlet as the true culprit. Hamlet has also regarded Claudius as the culprit where his own vengeance is concerned and has not acted against him; his own resolution in the matter of revenge begins when Laertes justly challenges him. He is indeed the murderer of Polonius, while Claudius is not, and from this moment in the play he is changed from a man who cannot act into a resolute man of action.

After the fashion of fantasy, the hero has not wholly divided off his acknowledged feelings from those which are unacknowledged and assigned to characters other than Hamlet. His drama concerns his own thoughts of parricide and usurpation, for which he believes death must be the punishment. In these circumstances the killing of Claudius alone could achieve no real revenge.[8] Hamlet feels that it is against himself that vengeance must be taken, and it will be this feeling that causes his paralysis. In preparing for his revenge, he must prepare his mind for his own death. A consideration of Hamlet's thoughts during the period of the delay (which forms most of the play) reinforces the conviction that he is preparing his mind for his own death. The theme of death is one of the play's most prominent themes – especially as it has been developed by the dramatist's imagination – and Hamlet's preoccupation with it climaxes in his best-known soliloquy and in the scene with the gravediggers.

It is after the scene in the graveyard that Hamlet's irresolution is replaced by a resolution to accept Laertes' avenging challenge. In the graveyard, Hamlet has brought himself face to face with his own death sentence and with the death of Ophelia, and now he is justly challenged as the killer of Polonius. While he could not act only against Claudius, he can agree wholeheartedly to Laertes' act of vengeance. In the light of the play's fragmentation of character and incident, Hamlet's new resolution can be seen to be due to his having at last undertaken his suicidal revenge. The avengers become engaged in an apparent mirror-image act of vengeance. That which is actually taking place is disguised through the use of Hamlet's other self, Laertes, and the second murdered father, Polonius.

Hamlet's revenge includes the need to dispatch all that Claudius represents, but he only kills Claudius when he knows that he himself is about to die at Laertes' hands. It must also be important that he has just witnessed the death of the queen, particularly as his witnessing the death of Ophelia immediately precedes his resolution to accept Laertes' challenge. Hamlet acquires the resolution to act in a matter concerning revenge on two ·occasions and each is immediately preceded by the death of one of the women. The significance of such a repetition cannot be ignored; but the motif of the women does not occupy as central a position throughout the play as does the theme of revenge, and it therefore seems that the news from Laertes that Hamlet has in him 'not half an hour of life' – which comes just after the death of the queen – is the news which brings the prince to dispatch Claudius.

Hamlet's treatment of Ophelia also makes sense if it is examined in the context of the fantasy structure which has been traced in the play. Ophelia is linked with Gertrude by the parallel character of the scenes in which they appear alone with Hamlet. Gertrude is involved in an incestuous relationship with Claudius, and while incest is barely mentioned in Hamlet's scene with the queen, he thinks of Nero when leaving to see her[9]: Nero, it is believed, was not only his mother's murderer but also her lover. He also accuses her of unfaithfulness to his father, and of showing unseemly lust for a woman of her age, with expressions of disgust which are reminiscent of the feelings which create the Loathly Lady. A similar disgust is expressed in Hamlet's scene with Ophelia, and while incest, not surprisingly, goes unmentioned in this scene, Hamlet's treatment of Ophelia only makes sense if he is thinking of incest. He behaves towards Ophelia as if he loves her but must renounce her. This is particularly clear in the scene Ophelia describes where Hamlet visited her in her closet in a 'piteous' state, seeming mad for her love. He gazed at her, drew a sigh which seemed to 'end his being' and then left the closet with his eyes still fixed on her. On another occasion, during the scene of the play-within-the-play, Hamlet seems to do the reverse of renouncing Ophelia, but here it can be discerned that in choosing her he is renouncing another woman, his mother:

GERTRUDE: Come hither my dear Hamlet, sit by me.
HAMLET: No good mother, here's metal more attractive.

There is no overt reason why Hamlet should renounce the daughter of Polonius. This obsession with incestuous love explains the presence of the spying and haunting fathers during the scenes when the prince is alone with Ophelia and Gertrude: a hero harbouring such thoughts would suppose their watchfulness.

It does appear that there is a coherent scheme present in the play, within which the play's strange features make sense, and this coherent scheme is evidently the creation of fantasy. The characteristics indicating the quality of the thought creating the plot are the puzzles which the play presents to the rational mind, the dreamlike fragmentation of character, and the fact that the plot only makes sense when it is understood to be the creation of the hero, as he contemplates his inner world using magical methods of thought. The fundamental characters appear to be a father, mother, sister and brother. The brother is the hero, and he appears – in separate characters – as both the usurper of the father's position and his father's avenger. Since the theme of the fantasy is usurpation and revenge, such motifs as parricide, incest and the consequent punishment by death of the hero are prominent in the play. The subject matter is typical of fantasy in being tortuous and still further complicated by disguise.

While the strange features of the play all make sense when considered within their context as elements in a fantasy structure, some of these features also make sense at other levels of thought in the play. Upon identifying the presence of a magical scheme in a work of literature, one has to bear in mind that a parallel, imaginative scheme may comprise some, or even all, of the same detail, and, in the case of *Hamlet*, there is a rich development of much of the thought in the fantasy structure. Since this aspect of the play has received abundant attention already, the present study need do no more than briefly show how the material created by the imagination relates to the fantasy structure. An examination of one half-scene – the gravediggers' scene[10] – will now be made for this purpose.

The gravediggers' scene shows how Shakespeare's imagination has dwelt on an incident in the fantasy structure and transformed it into a scene expressing a far-reaching vision of the drama of man's life. At the same time, the purposes of the fantasy find expression. At the level of fantasy, the hero is looking for a feeling that he can undergo his own death, and thus the gravediggers' insouciant discussion of the act of suicide, and the hero's accepting encounter with death, relate in part to the fantasy scheme. However, the detail in the scene can be seen to be engaged in a lively relationship with the other detail, not in order to develop fantasy motifs but in order to create a tragicomic vision of the life of man, together with a particular attitude towards this vision. The discussion to follow will briefly trace the material in the scene, and show that, while it relates in general to the fantasy scheme, it is concerned in almost all its particulars with the imaginative vision.

As the scene opens, the sexton and his fellow gravedigger are digging Ophelia's grave and discussing her suicide. Their discussion makes fun of an inquest law that can find a way of allowing a suicide a Christian burial because she had been a gentlewoman. The sexton then proves that gravediggers are gentlemen through claiming that they 'hold up Adam's profession' and he 'was the first that ever bore arms'; 'The Scripture says Adam digged' and 'Could he dig without arms?' Below the laughter at the contemporary scene and the enjoyment of the play on words and ideas, lies a fresh, lighthearted approach to the themes of suicide and death. Other jokes assert that suicide has to be a deliberate act and, through the linking of Adam with gravediggers, the jokes emphasize that death has always been with us.

The riddle that comes next stresses how much longer we are dead than anything we achieve on earth survives. Its answer declares that the gravemaker builds stronger than the mason, the shipwright and the carpenter because 'the houses he makes last till doomsday'. After this, the fellow gravedigger goes out to fetch the sexton a 'stoop of liquor' while the sexton digs and sings. His song is a garbled version of a lament absurd enough in itself, but through its nonsense can be discerned contrasting visions of time – the youthful lover's vision of time as an ally and the ageing man's vision of time as a stealthy enemy, annihilating the sometime lover 'As if [he] had never been such'. At this point the sexton throws up a skull. Hamlet and Horatio have entered, and Hamlet wonders that a gravedigger can have 'no feeling of his business, that 'a sings in gravemaking'. Horatio replies that 'Custom hath made it in him a property of easiness'. Contemplating the skull, Hamlet comments that it is treated as if it were the ass's jawbone with which Cain did the first murder; he adds that, while an ass may now be getting the better of it, it might once have belonged to a politician subtle enough to outwit God. Hamlet dwells further on the contrast between the skull without tongue or jaw, 'knocked about the mazzard with a sexton's spade', and the courtier, lawyer or buyer of land to which it might once have belonged. Next comes an exchange between Hamlet and the sexton:

> HAMLET: Whose grave's this sirrah?
> SEXTON: Mine sir . . .
> HAMLET: I think it be thine indeed, for thou liest in't.
> SEXTON: You lie out on't sir, and therefore 'tis not yours; for my part I do not lie in't, yet it is mine.
> HAMLET: Thou dost lie in't, to be in't and say it is thine. 'Tis for the dead, not for the quick; therefore thou liest.
> SEXTON: 'Tis a quick lie sir, 'twill away again from me to you.

Thus the merry wit over the grave continues. It is of moment, of course, that the grave actually belongs to Ophelia, but the play of wit over a grave also creates a vision of life central to the drama.

It is after this that the sexton answers Hamlet's question as to how long he has been a gravemaker.

> SEXTON: Of all the days i' th' year I came to't that day that our last King Hamlet overcame Fortinbras.
> HAMLET: How long is that since?
> SEXTON: Cannot you tell that? Every fool can tell that; it was that very day that young Hamlet was born . . .

This important statement is followed by jests, including the joke that all Englishmen are as mad as Hamlet. Finally, before Ophelia's funeral procession enters, Hamlet contemplates all that remains of the professional jester Yorick; and reflects that no woman can ward off this destiny through painting 'an inch thick', and that Alexander and Caesar might have ended up as earth stopping a hole in a beer barrel or in a wall 'to keep the wind away'.

In this scene Shakespeare's imagination has taken aspects of the fantasy theme of death the punishment for usurping ambition and transformed them into a searching reflection on the condition of man as a creature in nature and time. Somewhere between Adam and Doomsday, each individual has a brief moment above ground in which to assert himself, engage in evil, make love, jest, build, own land and get the better of God. After this he is extinguished. Within this vision of the individual's brief, assertive life, surrounded by non-existence, is a vision of the life-affirming gravedigger, to whom life is fun and death does not matter. His attitude contrasts strongly with the rejection and disgust expressed by Hamlet before he achieves a measure of acceptance in the graveyard. This scene plays a prominent role in the play's imaginative contemplation of attitudes to the living of a life which must be imperfect and under sentence of death.

The scene with the gravediggers has further, immediate appeal at the verbal level of thought. There is the broad joke that all Englishmen are as mad as Hamlet, while much of the humour combines the task of conveying the scene's imaginative and fantasy themes with the verbal appeal of riddles and punning. The scene is also full of reflections on contemporary society, including the practice of the law, the behaviour of courtiers and politicians, and the distinctions made between peasants and gentlefolk. Moreover, the detail appeals to our enjoyment of the macabre.

The thought creating this scene does not appear to have total control over all the material in it, for, at one point, detail meaningful at the level of fantasy, while puzzling at rational levels of thought, appears among the jests. The gravedigger suggests that three such disparate events as the beginning of his vocation, the killing of King Fortinbras and the birth of Hamlet all took place on the same day. Imaginatively, we may grasp that Hamlet has lived alongside death from the day of his birth, but why are death and his birth emphatically linked with his father's killing of an ambitious enemy? Moreover, why is a beginning of the digging of graves connected with the killing of this aggressor? The rest of the scene appears to be expressing a vision of death as being our destiny *in spite of*, not *because of*, what we do – with the important exception of suicide. The gravedigger's information does not link up meaningfully with the rest of the detail, and it is too extraordinary to make sense at the level of thought awakened by the rest of the exchange between the gravedigger and Hamlet.

In fine, the distinct fantasy and imaginative purposes of the scene can be seen to operate together in harmony. The imaginative purposes do not have a total, controlling grasp of the fantasy, and the fantasy, for its part, takes no cognizance of the activity of the imagination; but there is minimal confusion. There is, in fact, less material of a puzzling nature in this scene than in some other parts of the play, probably because the gravediggers are an invention of Shakespeare rather than material taken from the sources. While the scene is a stage in the progression of the fantasy, most of its detail is fundamentally the creation of the imagination.

II
The Source Material and the Play

As Geoffrey Bullough points out in his discussion of *Hamlet* in *Narrative and Dramatic Sources of Shakespeare*[11], there is no proof as to which of the available sources for the Hamlet story Shakespeare actually used. Saxo Grammaticus' Latin version in his *Historiae Danicae*[12] (dated about 1200 and printed in 1514) is one source which Shakespeare might have used: Saxo mingles the Northern legends of Amleth, oral and written, with the old Roman story of Lucius Junius Brutus. There was also Belleforest's French version of Saxo's story,[13] in his *Histoires Tragiques*, which appeared in 1576 and is more likely to have been read by Shakespeare; Belleforest both alters the story and adds material to it. Furthermore, there was an English drama of *Hamlet* – now no longer extant – in 1589, according to Nashe's address to 'The Gentlemen Students of Both Universities'.[14] Shakespeare undoubtedly knew this play, but we can only conjecture as to its content. There is a slight suggestion in Nashe's address that the earlier play was the work of Kyd, whose *The Spanish Tragedy*[15], a play with many superficial resemblances to the features of Shakespeare's play, might also have inspired Shakespeare. The dramatist would probably have known the Roman story of Lucius Junius Brutus, which appears in the first book of Livy's Roman History[16]: Brutus simulated idiocy in a situation similar to that of Hamlet, and his name expresses this idiocy – as probably does 'Amleth'[17], too, although Shakespeare would not have known it.

There is material from further sources, which might be guessed at with slightly more certainty. The idea of the method by which King Hamlet was murdered – which is enacted in the play-within-the-play of the Murder of Gonzago – was probably taken from Hoby's translation of Castiglione's *Il Cortegiano*[18], which appeared in 1561. This work contains an account of how Luigi Gonzaga, in 1538, poisoned Guidobaldo I of Urbino's heir and successor by pouring a lotion into his ears. The translation of Grimaldus Goslicius' *The Counsellor*[19], which appeared in 1598, was probably the source of the name and character of Polonius: written by a Pole, it is dedicated to the 'King of Polonia' and the translation delivers its rather trite suggestions in a verbose style. The name 'Claudius' must have been inspired by thoughts of the Emperor Claudius, who made an incestuous marriage. Julius Caesar's death is a source of inspiration in the play: it is likely that Shakespeare wrote *Hamlet* immediately after writing *Julius Caesar*. Shakespeare found inspiration, moreover, in contemporary events, such as England's dealings with Denmark and Poland, and the acts of piracy taking place in the North Sea[20]. He was, furthermore, profoundly inspired by contemporary thought – as he must be: the Northern hero is transformed into a Renaissance man of great intellectual activity.

Even while there is some uncertainty as to which the sources were, and we are not able to study the earlier *Hamlet*, it is still possible to give some illuminating consideration to Shakespeare's treatment of source material. It is particularly interesting to observe the features of the versions of the Amleth story given by Saxo and Belleforest: a resumé of these versions follows.

At the beginning of Saxo's and Belleforest's accounts, we are told that Amleth's father, Horwendil, and his uncle, Feng, have been appointed joint governors of Jutland by Rorik, King of Denmark. It appears also that Horwendil becomes king while Feng does not. After being king for three years, Horwendil goes roving and encounters Koll, King of Norway and renowned in arms, who challenges him. This king he kills in battle (in Saxo, hewing off his foot). Then he slays Koll's warrior sister, Sela, and plunders Norway. The pick of his plunder Horwendil gives to Rorik, and by thus currying favour with him, he marries Rorik's daughter, Gerutha. Amleth, their son, is born. Feng then slays Horwendil in his jealousy, and marries Gerutha himself. In both versions, the slaying is known rather than secret, and in Belleforest's version it takes place at a banquet; Saxo has Feng give as an excuse that Gerutha needed rescuing from Horwendil, while Belleforest has Gerutha Feng's lover before the murder.

Amleth feigns to be a dirty, listless simpleton, in order to save himself from Feng and also to achieve revenge. Unless Feng's fit of jealousy occurs much later than one would imagine, it seems that Amleth grows up pretending to be a simpleton. One day, he is observed making wooden hooks with steel barbs, using more skill than a simpleton could acquire. He says that they are javelins to avenge his father. A test is devised to discover the hero's true state of mind, and this test involves having a woman tempt him while watchers observe how he responds. The lure of the woman, it is argued, will overcome Amleth's powers of deception.

Saxo first gives an account of the journey to the tryst, which Belleforest leaves out. Amleth rides facing his horse's tail, and a wolf crosses his path amid the thicket. As he rides, Amleth makes witty answers to his companions' remarks, mixing wiliness with frankness. Passing along a beach, his companions find the rudder of a ship which has been wrecked and say they have discovered a huge knife. 'This', says Amleth, 'is the right thing to carve such a huge ham', meaning the sea. Passing sandhills and bidden to look at this 'meal', he replies that the sand has been ground small by the hoary tempests of the ocean.

In Saxo's account, the woman dispatched by Feng meets Amleth in a dark spot, as though she has crossed him by chance, and he takes her and would have ravished her if his foster brother had not given him an inkling of a trap. He warns Amleth that the woman is a snare by using a gadfly carrying a straw in its tail as a sign, and Amleth and the willing girl escape to make love in a fen in private. They are foster-brother and sister and therefore, in their friendship, agree to secrecy. When questioned later, the girl denies that Amleth responded to her, while he affirms in vain that he did, adding that he used as his pillow the hoof of a beast of burden, a coxcomb and a ceiling. Belleforest omits the gadfly and the fen, adds the lady's warning to the foster-brother's and, generally, gives a much more confused account of the incident, bringing out the ambiguities which Saxo leaves apparently unaltered, in folktale imagery such as the gadfly. Belleforest's treatment of the incident will be discussed later: suffice it to say now that we never learn from Belleforest whether Amleth and the girl make love; the hero is said to deceive the girl as well as the courtiers, and to maintain that he has not violated her, while also saying the contrary. In both versions of the story, it emerges at the tryst that the lady is well-known to Amleth: in Saxo, she is his foster-sister and in Belleforest she is a beautiful 'Damoyselle' who has loved the hero from her infancy.

Next, Feng absents himself while a friend (in Belleforest, a counsellor) carries out his own suggestion that he should eavesdrop on a meeting which Amleth has with his mother. Amleth, suspecting a spy, jumps about on the straw (in Belleforest, the quilt) in which he is hidden, proclaiming as a pretext for doing so a characteristic pretence that he is a cock, crowing and flapping his arms. Thus, he locates the eavesdropper, stabs him and drags him out to kill him. He next proceeds to chop him up, boil him and send him down the sewer to the pigs. Belleforest has Amleth also search his mother's room next door, distrusting her as well as the rest. In the ensuing tête à tête, Amleth upbraids his mother for committing incest with her husband's slayer, and eventually brings about her repentance. Belleforest has the queen say her marriage was enforced, which is a lie according to Belleforest's account of the earlier events. From now on, the queen is Amleth's ally. When Amleth tells the king and court the fate of the spy, they think he is speaking nonsense.

Feng's next device is to send Amleth to the king of Britain with two envoys who are bearing a letter requesting the British king to kill Amleth. Before leaving, Amleth instructs his mother to hang the hall with knotted tapestry and perform pretended obsequies for his death a year from that date. On the journey he finds the letter and alters it, making it request the execution of the envoys and the marriage of the king's daughter to the youth of great judgement being sent to him. In

Britain, Amleth shows remarkable powers of divination. To Saxo this is the sign of a hero and to Belleforest it is a characteristic of an inhabitant of a pagan land full of enchanters. Among his divinations, Amleth senses death in the bread and meat, and the rust of iron weapons in the drink. An inquiry proves that the corn for the bread has been grown, by design, in a field made fertile by slaughtered men, and the meat has come from hogs which strayed and ate the rotten carcase of a robber (in Belleforest, a hanged one); the water used in the drink has come from a spring containing rusted weapons. Saxo adds that some say the honey in the drink has come from bees which have been feeding in the paunch of a dead man. Amleth also declares that the king is of slave stock and the queen of low birth, and this is proved true. The king's interest in him is aroused, for he recognizes him as wise, and this interest culminates in Amleth's betrothal to the princess. The envoys are executed and Amleth, pretending ignorance of the letter, demands blood money. Then he melts down the gold and pours it into two hollow wands.

After staying in Britain a year, Amleth returns to Jutland and immediately goes to the court, making himself look filthy and absurd. According to his instructions, the court is celebrating his last rites, and all are terrified when he appears. Asked about the envoys, he says that they are in his sticks. He is full of jokes, which most think idle, and he takes round the drink. When he feels the point of his sword, bystanders nail it to its scabbard. Having made the lords drunkenly asleep, Amleth pulls down the hangings put up by his mother, covers everyone and binds them up inside with the hooks he has prepared. He then sets fire to the palace. Next, he goes to Feng, who is asleep, exchanges his useless sword and scabbard with Feng's and wakes him. Feng seizes what he believes to be his sword and cannot protect himself from death. Amleth then makes a long oration to the people, saying that Feng was not a prince but a fratricide and traitor who defiled his brother's queen, and set himself up instead of his brother as a tyrant. He asks that his mother should be pardoned and that he should become ruler.

Amleth is now avenged and becomes king, but his story does not end here. He returns to Britain to fetch his wife, only to have his father-in-law become his enemy, for he is under an oath of blood-brotherhood with Feng and must avenge his murder. He seeks to carry out his oath by sending Amleth to woo Queen Hermutruda in Scotland, on his behalf, without telling him that she kills all her suitors. Queen Hermutruda, however, takes a different view of Amleth. In Saxo, she sees the shield which he has had made, depicting the story of his subtle heroism and revenge, and thereupon changes the letter which Amleth is carrying for another requesting her to marry the bearer. Her crown will go with her hand, and Amleth complies. Belleforest characteristically omits the folktale imagery and trick, and has the queen desire Amleth without the aid of his life history, subtly persuading him to marry her while his ambition leads him to agree. On his return, his first wife accepts the situation and warns him that her father intends to kill him. Amleth then defeats Britain, largely through the strategy of setting up his slain comrades in battle array: the terrified Britons flee and are thus 'conquered by the deadmen whom they had overcome in life'. Belleforest omits this evocative detail. The king is killed, and Amleth returns to Jutland with his plunder and his two wives, the first of whom now has a son and still loves her husband.

Meanwhile, Rorik has died and Wiglek, who has succeeded him, is busy harassing Amleth's mother and stripping her of her wealth. He claims that Amleth has usurped the kingdom of Jutland, for the king of Leire has the sole privilege of giving and taking away the rights of high offices. Amleth gives rich presents to Wiglek, but then is brought to accept the challenge to war which destroys him. His final thoughts have been for Hermutruda, who swears not to survive him, but she gives herself to Wiglek as soon as Amleth is killed. In Belleforest, Hermutruda is treacherous before the battle, having 'intelligence' with Wiglek and a promise of marriage.

Saxo ends his version with a little moralizing on women, which Belleforest intensifies. Where Amleth is concerned, Saxo praises his successful revenge after he has recounted it, saying that it has been achieved by Amleth's subtle disguise of folly and his surpassing wisdom. Belleforest praises Amleth's virtue, courage and admirable character and says that his weakness has been women; his downfall has been brought about by his unbridled desire for Hermutruda. Such praise for Hamlet has been equalled by audiences of Shakespeare's play.

The following investigation of these two versions of Amleth's story will have the particular concern of exploring how Shakespeare re-creates the story, and it will also give special attention to the likely sources of his play's puzzling features. The investigation will trace the fantasy structure in the source material, and show how it is similar but distinct from that traced in Shakespeare's play. This structure has four fundamental characters: a killed-cum-killer king, a queen, a princess and a prince. The prince is the hero, and he is divided up into two key characters: the avenger of his father, opposed to the usurper, and the parricidal usurper of both kingdom and queen. The theme is the usurpation of the king's position and the consequent punishment by death. Unlike the play, the source material has a structure which extends into five moves.

A number of interesting features may be observed in both versions of the Amleth story. The first is that Amleth's father and uncle are appointed joint rulers, but his father becomes king, while the uncle is referred to, in Amleth's speech after his revenge, as if he were a subject (Amleth describes Feng as having overpowered the people's 'Roy legitime'[21]). There is no comment on this ambiguous situation, and one can only note that joint rulers occur elsewhere in Saxo (for example, Rorik's father made his sons, Herlik and Gerit, rulers of Norway) and Feng is not accused in Amleth's speech of being a usurper so much as a fratricide, incestuous defiler of the queen, and tyrant. This matter is important for *Hamlet* because Claudius is presented as a usurper, not as a surviving ruler by hereditary right, and one of the most striking features of the play is the position of the thirty-year-old prince, living at court as subject to a usurping uncle. In the seventeenth century Norway and Denmark came under the same ruler, a ruler elected by the German princes, and while, in Shakespeare's play, Norway and Denmark are separate kingdoms, the election system is reflected in Hamlet's words to Horatio:

> He that hath killed my king and whored my mother;
> Popped in between th' election and my hopes . . .[22]

Hamlet's 'hopes' are referred to on one other occasion in the play, when he tells Rosencrantz that his 'cause of distemper' is that he lacks 'advancement'. Rosencrantz asks 'How can that be, when you have the voice of the king himself for your succession in Denmark?' The king, however, has usurped the throne, not been elected: why should he have a voice, let alone retain the throne? There might be a confusion between the system given in the sources and the Danish system existing in Shakespeare's day, but this possibility reinforces the impression given by the play as a whole that the dramatist is not much concerned with these political factors; his interest lies elsewhere. Both systems are so different from the English system that they need to be explained, but there is no explanation in the play. Elizabethan audiences must have felt that Hamlet should be king, and Shakespeare is probably making dramatic use of this expectation; but the matter is touched upon remarkably seldom.

Another interesting feature is that in the Saxo and Belleforest versions, Amleth appears to *grow up* feigning to be dull. Again, this is not made particularly clear, but these versions, with their suggestion that Feng has a right to rule and Amleth is only a child – initially – do give a more credible account of events than does Shakespeare's play.

The first test of Amleth's mental condition has odd features and there is an interesting relationship between the account given by Saxo and that given by Belleforest. The observation of Amleth's response to the lure of a woman who has been reared with him is a strange test of a man's true state of mind, and even in Saxo's straightforward account the incident appears to be ambiguous. Amleth jokes about the gadfly after the tryst, saying that it wore a stalk of chaff fixed to its hinder parts: this suggests the reverse of its stated purpose to forestall dangerous lovemaking. Moreover, it is only after the lovemaking that we learn that the hero and the girl have been under the same fostering in their childhood and are therefore in great intimacy; the girl agrees heartily not to disclose their lovemaking to anyone for this reason. The events in Saxo's account of the journey along a beach to the tryst (which Shakespeare may well not have read) appear to be sexual images expressing thoughts in the mind of the hero as he contemplates the girl. The story has coherent form as a fantasy, and this sharpens the interest of the close relationship between the hero and the woman, which is not explicitly presented as a blood relationship, instead being disguised as a foster relationship. Saxo's explanation for the tryst – that passion in young men is too impetuous to be checked by cunning and therefore if Amleth is only feigning lethargy he will give himself away at the tryst – appears ambiguous too. It seems to mean that, if Amleth responds, he is not really lethargic; he is feigning. However, this must be a rationalization (one using the magical theme of deception), because the tryst is too extraordinary a test for listlessness. The magical meaning suggested by the context is that, if Amleth responds, the watchers will know he has a passion for the (forbidden) girl which his cunning deception cannot hide. His eluding the watchers for the enjoyment of his love makes sense at both levels of meaning.

Belleforest's more analytical treatment of the story leads to his becoming confused by the magical thoughts of incest lying beneath the rationalization (even as he presents the girl as a 'Damoyselle' rather than a foster-sister). His hero, like Saxo's hero, is being tested to see whether he is engaged in a deception ('tromperie'), but he adds a passage about the methods of testing, saying that they are stratagems often used in his own day, not to test whether the great are out of their senses, but to deprive them of strength, goodness and wisdom by means of leeches and devilish Lamias, these produced by their servants, the agents of corruption: 'artifices assez frequent de nostre temps, non pour essayer si les grands sont hors de leur sens, mais pour les priver de force, vertu et sagesse par le moyen de ses sansues et infernales Lamies, produites par leurs serviteurs, ministres de corruption'.[23] Belleforest seems to see something horrifying in the tryst, feeling that it is not so much to find out how much Amleth is out of his senses as to create a situation in which he will take leave of them. The words 'sansues' (leeches) and 'Lamies' (Lamias) both suggest bloodsuckers, and Lamia is a female monster who preys upon human beings. The suggestion is that responding to the woman will deprive the hero of strength, goodness and wisdom. Belleforest is recoiling from the story's magical meaning, and he returns to the rationalization in his account of Amleth's foster-brother's warning. The foster-brother gives details of the danger to Amleth, and from these we learn that if the hero shows any sign of good sense he will be in mortal danger, and he therefore must not respond to the woman's caresses. The suggestion here that responding to the woman's caresses will reveal good sense conflicts with Belleforest's earlier hint that it would be madness to respond; it also shows how much the use of 'lethargy', rather than 'simpleton', has aided Saxo's rationalization. Belleforest's analytical treatment leads to his presenting both levels of meaning in a state of confusion, while Saxo deals with them in the traditional fashion; the rationalization may not be very convincing but there is no confusion.

Belleforest's account of the test also ends in a number of ambiguities. We are told that the girl tells Amleth of the treachery because she has loved him from her infancy and would have been made distraught with grief over his misfortune — and yet more distraught to leave without enjoying the man she loves more than herself. We are also told that Amleth deceives the courtiers and the girl, maintaining that he has not violated the girl while he also speaks to the contrary. This contradiction convinces the courtiers that he is out of his senses. But why should such a contradiction do so? And what is meant by the detail that the girl would have been made more distraught by the loss of the lovemaking than by a disaster to Amleth? Furthermore, why are we told that Amleth deceives the girl as well as the courtiers? These confusing effects seem to have been created by the author's struggle to give a coherent, rational account of magical material. They seem also to arise from the author's attempts to transform a passage concerning thoughts of incestuous love into one describing the hero's virtuous behaviour. From this last comes the ambiguity as to whether or not the hero has made love to the girl; in Saxo only the watchers, not the audience, are left in doubt.

These are elusive matters, but this is the material which Shakespeare may well have contemplated, bringing both rational and magical thinking to bear, as he prepared his play. The girl concerned is a major source for the character of Ophelia, whose role in Shakespeare's play is particularly mysterious. As Geoffrey Bullough points out[24], Hamlet's motivation does not appear to have been thoroughly thought through where his relations with Ophelia are concerned.

The second test of Amleth's state of mind has features parallel to those in the first test. In both cases there is an attempt to spy on the hero while he is alone with a woman connected with him and thinking about sexual matters; the spying is arranged by the hero's uncle, the king. An examination of the second testing scene in the sources is also interesting because a pressing question in Shakespeare's play is the role of Polonius as eavesdropper: why is he spying on the queen's interview with her son – with her agreement? In Saxo and Belleforest it is, it seems, not with her agreement, although, in Belleforest, Amleth suspects his mother of complicity. The queen has also not called her son to her with a specific purpose, and it is made clear that the friend, or counsellor, is appearing instead of Feng himself because Feng is anxious that Amleth should not suspect his personal inquiry. The eavesdropping is undertaken to see whether Amleth behaves normally when away from the public eye. In the sources, the scene makes quite good sense. A notable point in this part of the story is that Amleth converts his mother into his ally and this is a feature in the First Quarto version of Shakespeare's play[25], which may well be an abridged and earlier version of Shakespeare's own composition.

From this stage onwards, the differences between Shakespeare's play and his likely sources increase. Most of the ensuing incidents in the sources are excluded in the play, but important elements apparent in them are to be found in it. The injured, patient princess of Britain is a source for Ophelia, and the fell Hermutruda, slayer of suitors, adored and faithless, seems not to have been excluded as Shakespeare pondered on his women characters. It is significant that he seems to bring her name together with that of Gerutha (they are 'Hermetrude' and 'Geruthe' in Belleforest) to form the name 'Gertrude'.[26] While affording no proof, this detail gives one a greater conviction that Shakespeare knew Belleforest's version.

Saxo's story, and also the material which Belleforest selected, throws light on *Hamlet*'s theme of death. In the play, it comes to its height in the gravediggers' scene, which does not appear in the sources. In the sources, thoughts of death haunt the hero as he seeks to prove himself worthy of the princess through the divinations; the dead men thought of are slain warriors and a punished thief. In Saxo, the hero also brings about the slaying of the king of Britain by creating an army of dead men. Here, there is a suggestion that Amleth conquers through joining forces with death, as arguably does Hamlet at the end of his drama. However, Amleth is not now dealing with revenge on his uncle; and, notably, it is not Amleth's revenge on his uncle which coincides with his own death, as in the case of Hamlet, but Wiglek's hostilities against him for himself being a usurper.

Some interesting patterns may be observed in the sources. The ambiguous position of Feng is a feature reinforcing the impression that here we have a situation created by the fantasy of the hero of the story. This impression is strengthened by the very name 'Feng', which must mean 'snatch' or 'seize'.[27] Feng, while being a father-figure to some extent, seems also to represent the hero himself, a disowned self who usurps the father's place. Another, acknowledged, aspect of the hero appears as a child, behaving like a child (as the cock imitation illustrates), seemingly unthreatening and secretly planning revenge. All the features of the story might be viewed as expressing thoughts of the hero as he contemplates, with ambivalent feelings, the idea of usurping his father's role.

In the events which do not appear in detail in Shakespeare's play, a situation parallel in certain respects with the events before Amleth leaves for Britain may be observed: Amleth is involved with another king at another court, with his daughter and, later, with another queen. The princess, like Saxo's foster-sister or Belleforest's 'Damoyselle', appears in a strange, parallel relationship with a queen; and the British king, like Feng, is declared unworthy of his throne (as the bastard son of a slave, in his case). Queen Hermutruda belongs, in a sense, and yet also does not belong, to the king. She belongs to him in the sense that the king wants her after his low-born wife has died (Saxo says that he wants her 'vehemently', while Belleforest makes him ambivalent), and she does not belong to him because she chooses Amleth. Gerutha similarly belongs and yet does not belong to Feng: she belongs because he wants and takes her and she does not belong because she really belongs to Horwendil, this first union precluding her subsequent belonging to someone else as closely related as Feng.

A pattern of five moves can be discerned. The first concerns Horwendil, who kills one king and thus gains the daughter of another, by giving him the pick of his plunder. This daughter is Amleth's mother. The first move ends with Feng's murder of Horwendil, and in the second move the acknowledged hero becomes Amleth. The third move begins with Amleth's transfer to Britain, and it includes his return to Jutland to kill Feng and take the throne. The fourth move begins with the return to Britain and includes the events in Scotland. The fifth move takes place in Jutland under the threat of Wiglek. In the initial move, Feng plays his ambiguous role of usurping hero and father-figure declared unworthy king.

The story as a whole concerns death as nemesis for the killing of a king, and the taking of his queen or daughter. Thus Horwendil kills Koll and gains Gerutha, only to die for it at Feng's hands; Feng kills Horwendil and gains Gerutha, only to die for it at Amleth's hands. Amleth kills Feng and does not gain Gerutha but, instead, the British princess, who is already won. He then becomes king. However, his princess's father now seeks to kill him for killing Feng, and this king's murder plan results in Amleth's theft of his queen; the two acts are seen as united in one act. Amleth then kills the king. Another king now seeks to destroy him and does so, taking his queen. The killer king is also a motif of the drama. Howendil, Feng, the British king, Wiglek and Amleth himself, for part of his drama, are all killer kings. The killer kings and the killed kings meld with each other to some extent: Horwendil is, in part, an aspect of the hero in the first move, and his drama parallels in miniature Amleth's own drama. Feng is both a king and not a king, and this is an ambiguity of key importance. In this ambiguous role, Feng is also an aspect of the hero, and is only wholly distinct from Amleth when the British king seeks to avenge his death. The kings of Norway, Britain and Denmark (Koll, Rorik, Wiglek and the fourth unnamed) play roles distinct from that of the hero. Koll and Rorik 'stand in' for each other, as also do Horwendil, Feng and the British king at times in the story. In the midst of all this confusion, it can be seen that the king of Denmark finally takes back what the hero had taken at the beginning of the drama: Wiglek, who kills Amleth and takes Hermutruda, is successor to Rorik, under whom Horwendil had killed Koll and thus acquired Gerutha.

The second move, it should be noted, ends when the hero has made his mother his ally against the incestuous killer of his father, who is also a threat to himself. In the third move, the hero demotes the king and queen, thinking as he does so of slain warriors, an executed thief and vanquished arms on which the royal pair now feast. However, he sees himself as proved correct and as winning the princess. It is then that Feng is disposed of and Queen Gerutha restored, while the hero becomes king. This, significantly, is not the end of the story. The princess has been the woman sought after in the third move, but she is not taken back to Jutland to be queen, and the hero returns to Britain. The reason for this entry into a new move becomes evident from its events. With thoughts of an avenging king, the hero's story must go on, and Hermutruda must be created. The winning of Hermutruda bestows more kingship on the hero, and the king's revenge is turned into the hero's further usurpation. The king is then overthrown but there is death in his overthrow, as Saxo vividly portrays, and the next and last move tells of this death, combined as it is with a return to the situation which existed at the beginning of the story.

It seems plausible to imagine that Shakespeare – or at least the writer of the earlier *Hamlet* play – knew Belleforest's version of the story, if not Saxo's, and grasping the whole fantasy profoundly, syncopated it for dramatic and other purposes. Shakespeare has taken the characters and action from the first and second moves, and from part of the third, leaving out much of the repetition of king, queen and young girl, but including the whole story in his vision. The syncope modifies the fantasy in a number of significant ways, but makes no major alteration.

First of all, Shakespeare's syncope, concentrating as it does particularly on the events of the second move, throws into emphasis the role of the hero as non-claimant to the throne. Whatever political reasons there may be for Hamlet's uncrowned status, the main reason is likely to be the same as that in the case of Amleth in his second move, that the hero has publicly assumed (in his acknowledged self, Hamlet) the role of non-usurper, on the side of the king and opposed to the usurper. The 'Feng' character plays the hero's disowned role of incestuous killer of the king, and seizer of the throne.

Shakespeare's syncope also throws into emphasis the famous delay, which in the original story carries little interest. In Saxo and Belleforest it appears, superficially, to have been necessitated by the hero's need to grow up physically before he can embark on revenge. However, the childhood of the hero is never sharply distinguished from his manhood. Significantly, the childhood emerges more as an idea than as an actual situation; the hero is playing with thoughts of being a loyal child. This interest changes after the second move. In the third move, the hero makes himself the husband of a princess, and as such disposes of Feng, restores his mother and makes himself king. In the fourth move, the hero makes a greater change, taking up his thoughts of the second move in a fresh guise, his acknowledged self, Amleth, becoming another 'Feng' in a situation where the rest of the characters are more disguised (not being presented as relatives). In the fifth move, Wiglek wreaks revenge on the hero as a usurper. While these events of the last three moves of the story do not appear in Shakespeare's play, their purport is present and becomes concentrated in Hamlet's delay, investing it with the meaning of the whole Amleth story. Hamlet is secretly planning revenge on the incestuous usurper of his father's position, but he himself is this usurper. The 'Feng' character is present in Claudius, but the punishment of Claudius is not enough: it is against himself that Hamlet's vengeance must be taken. This is why Hamlet's behaviour is that of a man faced with a paralysing dilemma. The revenge theme of the second move and the punishment of the fifth move have been compounded, this giving the revenge theme its startling character. Meanwhile, the focus on the second move has altered the presentation of the final vengeance as it appears in the sources: in both the sources and the play the hero punishes his usurping thoughts with death, but in the sources he appears as a victim while in the play he is the seeker of this vengeance.

With Shakespeare's emphasis on the delay, and his creation of a central theme of suicidal revenge, comes the elevation of the motif of death in the sources to a major theme of the play.

Shakespeare's syncope also gives prominence to the hero's assumed madness and to the spying motif. The ghost, which has been introduced into the play[28], has an interesting connection with these motifs: the hero of Shakespeare's version is not only spied upon; he is haunted by a murdered father. The murder is secret in the play, divulged to Hamlet alone by the ghost. And this secret disclosure initiates the action. In the sources the murder is known, and Amleth plays the role of secret avenger, one who is pretending to be a simpleton in order to save his life and to work unnoticed. In *Hamlet* the hero becomes an isolated man, secretly haunted by thoughts of a crime and by the vengeance which must be taken. As in the sources, there are two levels of madness, both magical. A witty madness becomes a cover for his activities against Claudius, while his inner drama as criminal and avenger is another kind of madness, remaining largely hidden and unexplained, but manifested in his scenes with Ophelia and in his melancholia. The mood of the play is conveyed in its opening scene, showing a single guard alone at night on the battlements where the ghost has been seen. When relieved, he says:

> For this relief much thanks, 'tis bitter cold,
> And I am sick at heart.

Shakespeare modifies the role of the women in the story. Structurally, he places Hamlet's scene with the queen in more obvious parallel with the earlier tryst than do the sources. Each meeting is spied upon by two father-figures (Claudius and Polonius, and Polonius and the ghost) and, in each, Hamlet tells the woman to renounce her sexuality. The theme of incest is intensified, particularly in the case of Ophelia, who becomes hedged about with thoughts of incest and horror. In Saxo, the nature of the family relationship between the hero and the girl is disguised (as a foster relationship), and the account of the tryst is untroubled by the thoughts of incest. Belleforest does penetrate the disguise a little and his sense of this danger in the tryst confuses his account. His treatment of the story may well have influenced Shakespeare's treatment of it.

While many of the 'repeat' characters in the sources do not appear in Shakespeare's play, those characters which are included are repetitive – creating a rather different pattern from that found in the source material.

Polonius is developed from a minor character in the second move, and he becomes an obvious aspect of the king character in the play. Hamlet thinks he is the king in the closet scene ('I took thee for thy better'), and it is significant that he is made father to Ophelia, as the British king is father to the princess in the sources, and as Horwendil is a kind of father to the girl in the second move (an idea obscured in Belleforest's version). Polonius' central importance as a murdered father has emerged clearly in the study of the play.

Laertes seems to be a development of the foster-brother in the sources, who warns Amleth that he is in danger at the tryst. Thus, like Polonius, Laertes is a development of a minor character in the second move. The foster-brother's relationship to the young girl in the move, and to the hero, have been profoundly grasped; the relationship to the girl is brought out into the open, whereas the relationship to the hero is given an important role in the drama, while remaining 'hidden' and understood only at the level of fantasy. During the study of the play, Laertes emerged as a 'repeat' character of Hamlet in a number of ways, most strikingly at the climax, when, in effect, he carries out Hamlet's suicidal revenge.

The study of the play has also suggested that Prince Fortinbras is a 'repeat' character of Hamlet. The Fortinbras pair, in fact, do not seem to be a development of any particular characters in the sources: links with the kings Koll and Wiglek are no more than superficial. Instead, they seem to express feelings in the fantasy which are left in need of expression by Shakespeare's concentration on the second move. They are solely concerned with the physical seizure of power (the very name means 'strong-arm'), while Hamlet plays out the role of a prince not concerned with seizing power. King Fortinbras is the unsuccessful aggressor linked with Hamlet in the words of the gravedigger, and Prince Fortinbras is the successful aggressor who becomes king. In the play, as in the sources, the theme of retribution is dominant, but in Prince Fortinbras the hero considers an alternative role that might be played. Moreover, dramatic convenience will not be the only reason for the final moment of the play, when Prince Fortinbras becomes king after Hamlet has carried out the retribution.

Shakespeare evidently brooded on the story of the Danish prince with all the powers of his mind. His fantasy was caught by the story's magical purposes, even as he also brought his imaginative art, intellectual interests and reading into play. The fantasy role of Polonius, for example, is developed alongside his development as a reflection on the Polish 'Counsellor', and the two purposes are united. At the fantasy level, Polonius is a father whom the hero has turned into a fool (even as Amleth turns the king in his third move into the bastard of a slave) and at the imaginative level other, satirical, purposes lead to the counsellor's being turned into a fool.

An interesting development can be seen in the roles of the women. Shakespeare has concentrated the story into a tragedy and one which breathes into the women tragic roles already hinted at in the role of the British princess. Gertrude is altered from an ally into a woman trapped by her own frailty, and Ophelia acquires the role of chief mourner for both the betrayal of lovers and the murder of fathers.

In conclusion, *Hamlet* appears, morphologically, to be a fantasy structure — to which all the substantial detail relates in some way — with a brilliant overlay created by the dramatist's imagination. As Shakespeare brooded on his source material, he made it uniquely his own, bringing to bear all levels of thought. The overlay includes imaginative insight into character and motive, and a searching into human dilemma and our ultimate condition — particularly in relation to our mortality. It also includes a sparkling wit, playing on words and on ideas culled from learning, philosophical inquiry and direct observation. There are brief, often humorous, considerations of matters such as theatre affairs, current books and ideas, and human behaviour.[29] The whole is written in the language which Shakespeare had achieved as he was entering his greatest period.

The dramatist's 'overlay' is fully integrated with the content of the fantasy structure, and never at odds with it, but it does not comprehend the entire structure. It does not, moreover, constitute a complete structure in itself: it is dependent on the fantasy structure. Some of the fantasy material — conspicuously the suicidal nature of the vengeance, the Prince's uncrowned status and the role of Ophelia — is left to have meaning only at the level of fantasy. Unintegrated into the play's imaginative scheme, this material lingers in prominent positions to puzzle us.

In *Hamlet* can be seen a great writer's engagement in the contemplation of a traditional fantasy and in its re-creation as an independent work; to this task he brings both his magical thought and his imagination. The result is powerful and satisfying from the point of view of entertainment, and it only raises problems when one seeks to study the play.

TOWARDS A CONCLUSION

The prime aims of this book have been to establish the important role of primitive, magical thinking (fantasy) in the creation of fiction, to distinguish this creative activity from imaginative art, and to demonstrate that the activity of magical thought in literature may be subjected to the same disciplined study as is appropriate in the case of imaginative art. The book has also made a limited exploration of the variety of ways in which writers may operate at the level of magical fantasy; while a traditional story may be created entirely by fantasy, fictional works of individual authorship which contain a fantasy usually show its operation combined with that of the imagination.

A particular difficulty I have had over explaining magical fictions is that Western minds tend to be trapped in consistent systems of ideas which do not include awareness of irrational thought systems or of the irrationality of some thinking believed rational. These consistent systems of ideas hang together in such a way that making a crack in them by showing an inconsistency is exceedingly difficult. In *Traditional Romance and Tale* and in articles[1] I have asked questions pointing out peculiar illogicalities in some of our stories, questions such as 'Why doesn't Sir Gawain realize the hideous old woman is his aunt?' and 'Why doesn't the talking horse in *The Goose-Girl* tell the king that the waiting-maid is an imposter *before* she sends him to the knacker?' Nevertheless, I find that readers still fit magical stories somehow into their systems of thought, even missing the fact that the stories are, in a sense, mad.

A good example of these consistent systems of thought, one which will do double duty since it can be seen by outsiders to be entirely magical, is given in E. E. Evans-Pritchard's *Witchcraft, Oracles and Magic among the Azande*.[2] Among the Azande, witchcraft is an ordinary, everyday reality. If a person suffers a misfortune, the reason why he has suffered it is that someone has bewitched him. He consults an oracle to identify the person, bringing forward the names of those he suspects of bearing him ill will. The person the oracle names nearly always accepts the verdict and, anxious to restore good relations, performs a ritual act of repentance. If this does not reverse the bad magic, it is assumed that he is not genuinely repentant or that a new witch is at work. If the accused person does not accept the verdict, the oracle may not have been performed correctly (perhaps a taboo was not observed) or it may have been deflected from the straight path by witchcraft. There is always an explanation within the magical system of thought, and, moreover, the magical system hangs together with the Azande's rational observations of the world: a bad potter will not be thought the victim of witchcraft when his pots split and, when a man's torch of lighted straw ignites his thatch, this is recognized as the immediate cause, while someone's hostility is the ultimate cause. Rational thought systems (which include the irrational) can show the same closed-circuit character, which precludes the recognition of internal contradictions.[3]

Our attempts to deal with magical stories as stories which must make sense in some way to our rational minds lead us to treat them as symbolic or metaphoric, expressing the ideas and observations of folklorists, depth psychologists, literary critics, sociologists and others. We have resisted facing the possibility that they are the creation of an irrational system of thought and have immediate, crazy purpose at the level of the narrative. Thus, ironically, we make these spontaneous expressions of feeling much more difficult than many a genuinely imaginative tale, and too abstract for the ready, wide acceptance they have enjoyed and, in the case of traditional stories, for their faithful transmission. Compounded with the problem that we can always find an explanation within our rational systems of ideas for the strange features of fantasy is the problem that fantasy combines being rarely scrutinized with being too familiar to us. It is too easy to rationalize its manifestations and fail to ask obvious questions about their absurdity. Where a fantasy has been so treated by accompanying imaginative thought that its absurdities have been given a superficial appearance of good sense, it is too easy to study the imaginative treatment and ignore the fantasy.[4]

Magical stories are difficult to study, because magical thinking is alien to the rational mind and often hard for that level of thought to follow, being confused and tortuous, often multiple in meaning and inclined to employ disguises. The task I have undertaken is the formidable one of finding the spontaneous, magical level of thought creating a particular fantasy and adopting it myself, while, at the same time, checking every step carefully, in the light of the contextual evidence. The discipline has to be rigorous, even as one simultaneously frees one's mind totally from that intellectual process, in order to engage in the story magically. The checking process emphasizes interpretation almost as much as do the symbolizers of stories, but I am much more interested in the *behaviour* of magical thinking as it creates a fiction. While I am always doubtful about my accuracy in understanding the complex purposes of any particular fantasy, I am certain of the validity of many of my observations concerning the magical creative process. In order to make these observations as accurately as possible, I have concentrated on the study of single works, containing a complete fantasy *structure*, since only a complete fantasy provides sufficient contextual evidence for analysis.

A summary of my findings as to the behaviour of magical thought when creating a story must be incomplete, as each magical fantasy is both complex and unique. However, for the convenience of readers, I will give the central points here. Each fantasy has to be seen as the creation of its hero or heroine – and of participants in the story, identifying with him or her. Its theme is the hero's feelings, which are usually in conflict, and it unfolds as the hero gives play to these feelings and seeks to solve their conflict. As the hero thinks, he uses a level of thought free from the laws and realities of the outer world and therefore having special powers to bring things about; these things are brought about in the mind alone, but the hero does not see this as a limitation because he is in a state of mind where the world beyond the self does not exist. The hero's thoughts spontaneously become his story's characters and events, and the magical power of every thought creates its excitement and fear, especially where there is conflict. The protagonist, meanwhile, may seek to gain control over the magic and bestow greater power upon the feelings he wishes to win by investing special magical power in rituals, words or objects. This, however, may not be necessary, as the hero may, like the hero of *Hamlet*, be able to organize events and characters so that a solution can be achieved, without having to overcome opposing feelings with additional magic. Some fantasies have little conflict impeding a solution: *She* and *The Ugly Duckling*, in their different ways, are an exploration of unwanted feelings which finally become changed to their opposite, when, it seems, the hero wishes for this change; *Jack and the Beanstalk*[5], moreover, is simply a celebration of wanted feelings. A fantasy advances in a cyclical fashion, as the hero repeats his enactment of his feelings, and, in a fantasy expressing much conflict, there may be many such repetitions, the hero varying his approach as he explores his feelings and seeks a solution. These cycles of thought, which I call moves, give the magical story a morphology quite distinct from imaginative story forms.

In fictions of individual authorship, rational and imaginative thought will usually work on magical material: at its simplest, this treatment amounts only to rationalization, while, where it is more thorough, a fantasy may be partly or wholly transformed by an author's imagination. The purposes of the transforming activity are very different from those of the fantasy, so there is a danger of discord or ludicrous effects; nevertheless, the two levels of thought may operate in harmony, and have done so in great works of literature. They may co-operate in a variety of ways, and, in particular, there can be an effective relationship between the feelings in the magical story and the author's imaginative purposes.

When writing *Traditional Romance and Tale*, I was interested in the relationship between magical story creation and dreams, while, in this book, I have been more interested in fantasy as ritual. Both approaches are useful: dreams are inconveniently elusive and obscure, but they help us to grasp the magical level of thought; ritual, meanwhile, is another manifestation of magical thinking well known to us, and it is an important – though not essential – feature of magical story creation. When I came to study non-traditional fictions, and found myself exploring the differences between magical thought and the imagination, I learnt more about the behaviour of magical thought, with the result that this is a fuller study; I also acquired the scope to explain this level of thinking and its activity more clearly, thus, I hope, leaving fewer loopholes for misunderstanding.

My inquiry into magical storytelling is confined to what is revealed by the evidence of the texts: I have not pursued those matters demanding evidence beyond the texts. Audience research should answer important questions still outstanding. The evidence of the texts suggests that the purposes of a fantasy accepted by audiences will be transmitted faithfully in oral and literary tradition, but this does not mean that every member of an audience has to grasp these purposes. There must be circumstances in which members of the audience decide not to participate in a fantasy. While magical thought knows no cultural or educational barriers, the desire to participate or opt out may be affected by sex, age or personal idiosyncrasies; emotional, rather than intellectual, ability must often be a deciding factor. In particular, what do girls and women make of hero stories dealing with apparently exclusively male experience, and vice versa? Do they, instead, treat the fantasy freely, creating their own stories from elements in the original? And so forth. Audience research would have to be carried out with the knowledge that people tend to rationalize fantasy continually, once there is any attempt to lift it from the storytelling situation. Moreover, the disguises should be retained in the case of children and adults with little literary sophistication.

The study of magical thought in fiction opens a door to new explorations for those concerned with fiction and audiences. One matter which must be stressed finally is the value of magical stories and plots. While a fantasy demands a quite different mental engagement on the part of audiences from that demanded by imaginative fiction – one which might seem not to extend the mind or experience – it should not be dismissed: it is clear that fantasy meets an important need and can be both challenging and emotionally nourishing.

It is my hope that magical fantasy will no longer be neglected and that the methods of study I suggest will contribute towards a fuller and deeper understanding of the creation and enjoyment of fictional literature.

NOTES

PREFACE

1. Anne Wilson, *Traditional Romance and Tale* (D. S. Brewer, Ipswich, 1976).
2. I discuss Ernest Jones in note 1 to Chapter 7. An interesting example of Freud's own work is to be found in his *Collected Papers*, Vol. IV (London, 1925), pp. 236–56, where he discusses 'Material from Fairy-Tales in Dreams' and 'The Theme of the Three Caskets'.
3. I discuss Bruno Bettelheim in my Introduction.
4. See particularly Keith May, *Out of the Maelstrom* (Paul Elek, London, 1977).
5. Derek Brewer, 'The Interpretation of Dream, Folktale and Romance with Special Reference to *Sir Gawain and the Green Knight*', *Bulletin of the Modern Language Society*, 4 LXXVII, 1976 (Helsinki); '*The Lord of the Rings* as Romance' in *J. R. R. Tolkien, Scholar and Storyteller* (see Chapter 4 in the present book and note 3 to Chapter 4); 'The Battleground of Home' in *Encounter*, April 1980; *Symbolic Stories* (D. S. Brewer, Ipswich, 1980). Dr Brewer is interested in the symbolism of stories, and has explored many as symbolic representations of the *rites de passage* from childhood to the freedom of the world outside the family.
6. Stephen Prickett, *Victorian Fantasy* (Harvester Press, London, 1979). Dr Prickett explores how the 'idea of fantasy' developed as an 'art form' during the nineteenth century and how E. Nesbit's curtain between 'the world of magic' and 'the world that seems to us to be real' was sometimes breached (pp. 12, 34).
7. Robert Scholes, *The Fabulators* (Oxford University Press, New York, 1967), p. 11.
8. Ibid., p. 136.
9. Ibid., p. 12.
10. Tzvetan Todorov, *The Fantastic* (Editions du Seuil, 1970; Cleveland: Press of Case Western Reserve University, 1973), pp. 107ff.
11. Vladimir Propp, *Morphology of the Folktale* (University of Texas, Austin, 1968).
12. Tzvetan Todorov, see note 10 above, pp. 163–4.
13. Tzvetan Todorov, *Grammaire du Décameron* (The Hague, 1970).
14. See particularly Claude Lévi-Strauss, *The Raw and the Cooked* (1964 and Cape, London, 1969).
15. Tzvetan Todorov, *The Fantastic*, p. 110.
16. Barbara Hardy, *Tellers and Listeners* (Athlone Press, London, 1975), p. 28.

INTRODUCTION

1. This quotation is the complete version of *The Goose-Girl* as it appears in the edition of *Grimm's Fairy Tales* published by Routledge and Kegan Paul (1948). The translation is a revision by James Stern of Margaret Hunt's translation, and the story is given its standard number, 89. This is one of a large number of translations of the collection of folktales made by the Brothers Grimm, which first appeared in the following edition: *Kinder- und Haus-Märchen, Gesammelt durch die Brüder Grimm* (Berlin, 1812–15). 2 vols. The Grimm brothers' version was one of many versions extant at the time during which they made their collection. See J. Bolte and G.

Polivka, *Ammerküngen zu den Kinder- und Hausmärchen der Brüder Grimm* (Leipzig, 1912–32), 3 vols., in which *The Goose-Girl* appears as *Die Gänsemagd*, no. 89, in Vol. 2, p. 273.

2. H. C. Andersen, *Eventyr og Historier*, i udvalg ved Hans Brix, Gyldendalske Boghandel, Nordisk Forlag, 1953. This edition is based on the first edition of Andersen's complete works. The English translation recommended by H. C. Andersens Hus (House), Odense, Denmark, is R. P. Keigwin, trans., *The World Edition of Hans Christian Andersen's Fairy-Tales* (4 vols.). Keigwin's 'The Ugly Duckling' has been published in Britain by Kaye and Ward, 1971. Another good translation is Erik Christian Haugaard's *The Complete Fairy Tales and Stories of Hans Christian Andersen* (Gollancz, London, 1974).

3. Victor Shklovsky, *Sur la Théorie de la Prose* (Lausanne, 1973; first published in Russia, 1929). Discussed briefly by Robert Scholes, in his *Structuralism in Literature* (Yale University Press, New Haven and London, 1974), pp. 83–5.

4. Russell Hoban, Introduction to *Household Tales by the Brothers Grimm* (Picador, London, 1977). By contrast Russell Hoban's novel *Riddley Walker* (Picador, 1980) captures precisely the magical level of thought and its perennial creation of myth and ritual.

5. Northrop Frye has likewise been concerned with mythic patterns in literature: he presents a theory of literature in which Demeter and Proserpine, for example, can be shown to appear in displaced form in many works (*Anatomy of Criticism*, Princeton University Press, New Jersey, 1957, pp. 138, 106). Myth he regards as the verbal communication of ritual and dream, but he sees the use of mythic patterns as the activity of the metaphoric imagination; he does not explore magical purpose in traditional storytelling. In *The Secular Scripture* (Harvard University Press, Massachusetts and London, 1976), p. 166, he offers an explanation as to how a mythic story might work among audiences. He suggests that the audience recognizes the mythic convention behind the alleged 'reality' of the story, and sends out 'imaginative roots into that mysterious world between the "is" and the "is not" ', where individual participants can journey towards their own identity. Frye's work on imaginative stories is useful; the problem lies in the assumption that a story is imaginative. I discuss the use of Frye's approach, together with the metaphoric and symbolist approaches in general, in relation to the nineteenth-century story *The Basket of Flowers* by Christoph von Schmid, in *Signal: Approaches to Children's Books*, no. 38, May 1982.

6. Bruno Bettelheim, *The Uses of Enchantment* (New York, 1976, and Penguin Books, 1978), pp. 136–44. I do not agree with Jack Zipes (in his *Breaking the Magic Spell*, Heinemann Educational, London, 1979) that Bettelheim's approach is 'pathetic and insidious' (p. 173). Zipes turns his back on Bettelheim's Freudian insights in pursuit of his own theory that folktales are 'part of humankind's own imaginative *and* rational drive to create new worlds that allow for total autonomous development of human qualities' (pp. 22–3); he believes their concerns are social and political. While this is an interesting notion, Zipes' methods are less satisfactory than Bettelheim's: unlike Bettelheim, he does not conduct a systematic inquiry into particular stories as part of his argument; and he rejects Bettelheim's insights without asking the obvious questions which many folktales raise. What are our answers worth if we fail to spot the questions they leave unanswered?

7. 'The Hare and the Well', in *Tales of Old Malawi*, by E. Singano and A. A. Roscoe (Popular Publications, Limbe, Malawi, 1974), is a good example of an African trickster story. The animals make a well, to cope with drought, and the hare does not help, although he wishes to benefit from it. To prevent his using the well, the animals take turns to guard it, but the hare gets water by offering the guard honey which can only be eaten if one is tied to a tree. Finally, the tortoise catches him by putting a sticky mixture on his back and pretending to be a stepping stone by the well. The hare tells the king, the elephant, to kill him by grabbing his tail and hitting him hard on a pile of sand. 'I'm tired of life anyway and I don't mind dying

today.' The elephant tries to hold his tiny tail and the hare slips away deep into the forest.
8. See Sallie TeSelle, *Speaking in Parables* (SCM Press, 1975). The parable of the Prodigal Son is a metaphor of God's love, which brings its audience to an awareness of this love through the details of the story. The response would not be to allegorize it: Is the father God? Is the feast a symbol of the kingdom? The order of perception in a parable is such that it keeps the audience's eyes on their familiar world rather than on God himself, and the new awareness comes from the transformation of that familiar world by the narrator's vision of God.
9. R. L. Stevenson, *Treasure Island*, first published in 1883, Chapter 26.
10. May Sellar's translation in *The World's Best Fairy Tales* (Reader's Digest Association, London, 1970).
The original German is:

> 'bis ich mich geflochten und geschnatzt,
> und wieder aufgesatzt.'

11. See Anne Wilson, *Traditional Romance and Tale*, p. 53 (note 2), on *The Golden Bird*, and also Chapter 6, part I, of this present book.
12. J. Bolte and G. Polivka, as in note 1 above, Vol. 2, p. 274.
13. Ibid., Vol. 2, pp. 278ff.
14. See Anne Wilson, *Traditional Romance and Tale*, pp. 53 (note 2), 71 (note 10), and also Chapter 6, part I, of this present book.
15. See J. Bolte and G. Polivka, as in note 1 above, Vol. 2, pp. 275ff.
16. By 'move' Propp means a repetition of the story sequence of leaving home, adventures, victory, return and recognition, which occurs when a fresh act of villainy creates a new initial lack in the home situation.
17. See Anne Wilson, *Traditional Romance and Tale*, pp. 15, 29, for a fuller discussion of this characteristic of fantasy.
18. In connection with this, it is interesting to note that W. H. Auden, in his essay 'The Guilty Vicarage' in *The Dyer's Hand and Other Essays* (Faber and Faber, London, 1963), sees detective stories as having a ritual, magical function: the detective story addict restores himself to a state of 'innocence' by means of having a genius from outside remove the suspicion of guilt, giving knowledge of it and expelling it.

CHAPTER
[1]

1. H. Rider Haggard, *She* (1887), now available in Coronet Books (1976).
2. See Anne Wilson, *Traditional Romance and Tale*, pp. 34–46, for the stories of *Cat-Skin* and *The Golden Bird*, which also illustrate the threefold action sequence in the place of adventure.
3. For a full discussion of this Grimm story, see ibid., pp. 20–31, 56.
4. Ibid., pp. 30–1, 44–6, 92.
5. For *The Weddynge of Sir Gawen and Dame Ragnell*, see Chapter Five.
6. *She* (Coronet paperback), p. 114.
7. Ibid., p. 68.
8. Ibid., p. 235.
9. Ibid., pp. 160, 118, 161.
10. Ibid., pp. 193–4.
11. Ibid., p. 206.
12. Ibid., p. 132. Marie-Louise von Franz interprets 'She' as the anima in the role of guide and mediator to the inner world (in Carl G. Jung, *Man and His Symbols*, Aldus Books, London, 1964, p. 186). The anima is defined as a personification of all feminine psychological tendencies in a man's psyche. In this case, we would understand 'She' to be an aspect of the hero rather than his vision of someone

'other'. However, a magical vision of someone 'other' is likewise a projection of one's inner world, so this matter becomes a minor problem of interpretation which would not contribute much to my examination of the story's function.
13. These examples from the Amahaggar scenes are to be found ibid., on pp. 71, 85 and 93 respectively.
14. Ibid., p. 150.
15. Ibid., pp. 214–5. The danger of a woman unveiling is also expressed on pp. 128, 131, with reference to 'She', and on p. 132, as a general comment.
16. Ibid., p. 197n.
17. Ibid., p. 122.
18. Ibid., pp. 207–8.
19. Ibid., p. 59.

CHAPTER
[2]

1. Charlotte Bronte, *Jane Eyre* (1847).
2. *King Horn*, edited by Joseph Hall (Oxford, 1901). The text used in this book is the London text.
3. See *Traditional Romance and Tale*, pp. 59–62.
4. See ibid., p. 59. Examples are *Tristan* (see the translation of A. T. Hatto, Penguin Books, 1960); *Havelock* (see the edition of W. W. Skeat and R. Sisam, Oxford, 1915), and *William of Palerne* (edited by W. W. Skeat, for the Early English Text Society, EETSES 1, London, 1867). I discuss *Tristan* in *Traditional Romance and Tale*, pp. 46–52.
5. See ibid., pp. 39–46, particularly pp. 45–6. There is a more recent, fuller discussion of this folktale in my article in *Signal: Approaches to Children's Books*, no. 36, September 1981 (Volume 12).
6. *Jane Eyre*, Chapter 6.
7. Ibid., Chapter 8.
8. Ibid., Chapter 13.
9. Adrienne Rich, *On Lies, Secrets, and Silence* (U.S.A., 1979, and Virago, London, 1980), pp. 89–106.
10. *Jane Eyre*, Chapter 27.
11. Ibid., Chapter 21.
12. During my discussion of the seventh move, I quote from Chapters 34 and 35.
13. *Jane Eyre*, Chapter 37.
14. Ibid., Chapter 34.
15. Some elements of the fantasy in this novel are strikingly similar to the fantasy to be found in Daphne du Maurier's *Rebecca*, where the heroine is also haunted by the feeling that she is only a child and that her married home belongs to another woman, her husband's first wife. This wife appears in the person of Mrs Danvers, who is described as if she were dead. After a series of attempts at exorcism, the haunting is finally exorcised by Mrs Danvers' burning the house down. I discuss this novel in my article in *Signal: Approaches to Children's Books*, no. 36, see note 5 above.

CHAPTER
[3]

1. For editions of H. C. Andersen's fairy tales, see note 2 to Introduction.
2. H. C. Andersen, *Eventyr og Historier*, see note 2 to Introduction, p. 304.

CHAPTER
[4]

1. J. R. R. Tolkien, *The Lord of the Rings*, published by Allen and Unwin in three parts: *The Fellowship of the Ring* (1954); *The Two Towers* (1954); *The Return of the King* (1955). The second edition appeared in 1966 and the paperback volume in 1968.
2. Randel Helms, *Myth, Magic and Meaning in Tolkien's World* (Thames and Hudson, 1974, and Panther Books, 1976).
3. Derek S. Brewer, '*The Lord of the Rings* as Romance' in *J. R. R. Tolkien, Scholar and Storyteller*, ed. Mary Salu and Robert T. Farrell (Cornell University Press, Ithaca and London, 1979), pp. 249ff.
4. Randel Helms, op. cit., in the publication of Panther Books (1976), p. 68.
5. Ibid., pp. 77–85.
6. Ibid., p. 92.
7. See ibid., p. 75.
8. Ibid., p. 92.

CHAPTER
[5]

1. Geoffrey Chaucer, 'The Wife of Bath's Prologue and Tale', edited by F. N. Robinson in *The Complete Works of Chaucer* (Oxford University Press, no date); also edited by James Winny in *The Wife of Bath's Prologue and Tale* (Cambridge University Press, 1965). Translated by Nevill Coghill in *The Canterbury Tales* (Penguin Books, 1951).
2. For studies and surveys of the Loathly Lady story, see the following: G. L. Maynadier, *The Wife of Bath's Tale* (London, 1901; Grimm Library XIII); L. Sumner (ed.), *The Weddynge of Sir Gawen and Dame Ragnell* (1924), Smith College Studies in Modern Languages, Vol. V, no. 4; G. B. Saul, *The Wedding of Sir Gawain and Dame Ragnell* (New York, 1934); J. W. Beach, *The Loathly Lady* (an unpublished dissertation, 1907, in the Harvard University Library); Sigmund Eisner, *A Tale of Wonder* (Wexford, 1957, and New York, 1969).
3. See Arthur C. L. Brown, *The Origin of the Grail Legend* (Harvard University Press, 1943), p. 216, where he shows how the grotesque exaggeration of Chrestien's language, when describing the Loathly Lady in his 'Conte del Graal' (or 'Percival', ed. William Roach, 1956, ll. 4614–37), resembles that in the Irish 'Dindshenchas of Carn Máil' (translated by Edward Gwynn, in *The Metrical Dindshenchas*, Part IV, Royal Irish Academy Todd Lecture Series, Vol. XI (Dublin, 1924), pp. 136–43; found in the 'Great Book of Lecan', compiled in 1417). The possibility that Chaucer had access to the Irish sources is also discussed by Sigmund Eisner in *A Tale of Wonder*, see note 2; this study argues that Chaucer's seeming alterations to the tale were taken from tradition.
4. John Gower, 'Confessio Amantis' in *The Complete Works of John Gower*, edited by G. C. Macaulay, Vol. 2 (Oxford, 1901), pp. 74–86. 'The Tale of Florent' is also edited by W. F. Bryan and G. Dempster, in *Sources and Analogues of Chaucer's Canterbury Tales* (Chicago, 1941), pp. 224–35.
5. 'The Weddynge of Sir Gawen and Dame Ragnell', edited by W. F. Bryan and G. Dempster, see note 4 above, pp. 242–64. This romance is briefly discussed in *Traditional Romance and Tale*, pp. 88–90.
6. 'The Marriage of Sir Gawaine', edited by W. F. Bryan and G. Dempster, see note 4 above, pp. 235–41.
7. The story of Lughaid Laeighe from the early fifteenth-century 'Book of Ballymote', edited by S. H. O'Grady, in *Silva Gadelica* (London, 1892), Vol II, Irish text pp. 489–90; English translation pp. 537–8.
8. 'Cóir Anmann' (Fitness of Names), translated by Whitley Stokes in *Irische Texte*, 111, 2 (Leipzig, 1897), pp. 316–23.
9. 'Dindshenchas of Carn Máil', see note 3, pp. 136ff.

10. 'Temair Breg, Baile na Fían', poem by Cuán ua Lothcháin (d. 1024), translated by Maud Joynt, in *Ériu*, 4 (Dublin, 1910), pp. 91–111.
11. 'Echtra mac Echach Muigmedóin', from the 'Yellow Book of Lecan', edited and translated by W. Stokes, in *Revue Celtique*, XXIV (Paris, 1903), pp. 190–203, and also translated by Myles Dillon in *The Cycles of the Kings* (London and New York, 1946), pp. 38ff. This version also appears in the 'Book of Ballymote', and it is edited and translated from this source by S. H. O'Grady in *Silva Gadelica*, see note 7, Irish text pp. 326–30; English translation pp. 368–73.
12. Ananda K. Coomaraswamy in *Speculum*, October 1945 (Vol. 20, no. 4), pp. 391ff.
13. An example of a *Fiers Baiser* story is *Libeaus Desconus*, edited by M. Mills, Early English Text Society 261 (1969). This story is discussed briefly in *Traditional Romance and Tale*, pp. 85–8.
14. Arthur C. L. Brown, as in note 3 above, Chapter 7, 'The Hateful Fée who Represents the Sovereignty'.
15. Proinsias MacCana, *Celtic Mythology* (Hamlyn, London, 1970), p. 117.
16. Ibid., p. 120.
17. The Wife tells us that her 'entente is nat but for to pleye' (Prologue, l. 192), and her shock tactics in her Prologue ll. 154–5 are a good example of her teasing.
18. There is an ironic relationship between the Wife's account of her subjugation of her fifth husband and her account of the subjugation of the knight. The former involves violence, trickery and the destruction of the husband's book.
19. Margaret Schlauch, in 'The Marital Dilemma in the *Wife of Bath's Tale*', PMLA, LXI (1946), pp. 416–30, relates Chaucer's alteration to the Wife of Bath's accusation in her Prologue that her old husband believes a woman cannot be beautiful and faithful (Prologue, ll. 253–6).

CHAPTER [6]

1. *Sir Gawain and the Green Knight*, edited by J. R. R. Tolkien and E. V. Gordon (Oxford University Press, 1925); second edition by Norman Davis (1967). There is also an edition by R. A. Waldron (Edward Arnold, London, 1970), and an edition with a translation by W. R. J. Barron (Manchester University Press, 1974). A translation by Brian Stone has been published by Penguin Books, 1959. Furthemore, *Sir Gawain and the Green Gome*, prepared by R. T. Jones (Heinemann Educational, London, 1972), gives the romance in its original language with regularized spelling, which makes the work accessible in the original to non-specialists.
2. See *Traditional Romance and Tale*, pp. 96–107, 80–3 and 1–6 passim.
3. *The Grene Knight* is to be found in Bishop Percy's Folio MS. *Ballads and Romances*, Vol. 2, edited by J. W. Hales and F. J. Furnivall (London, 1868), pp. 58–77. There is a translation of *The Grene Knight* into modern English by Elisabeth Brewer in *From Cuchulainn to Gawain: Sources and Analogues of 'Sir Gawain and the Green Knight'* (D. S. Brewer, 1973), pp. 83–91.
4. J. Burke Severs, *A Manual of the Writings in Middle English, 1050–1500*, Vol. 1 (New Haven, Connecticut, 1967), pp. 57–8.
5. *The Grene Knight*, ll. 52–4.

> shee cold transpose knights & swaine
> like as in battaile they were slaine,
> wounded both Lim & lightt.

Elisabeth Brewer, see note 3 above, translates these lines as 'She could change knights, as if they had been slain in battle, wounded both in limb and body, into peasants.' I am not happy with this translation, since, while it gives a more accurate translation of 'transpose', I think it makes less sense in the context of the story.

'Transpose', moreover, clearly means 'transform' in this romance: see its use to mean that the Green Knight transforms himself, 'he transposed him in another array' (l. 443).
6. Ibid., ll. 58–72.
7. I have followed Elisabeth Brewer's translation here; F. J. Furnivall, see note 3 above, has 'boldly', not 'body', so that the sense is that Gawain should take the lady boldly in his arms (l. 376).
8. The word used for 'look' is 'blush' – 'Sir Gawaine blushed on the Lady bright' (l. 382) – and the word also carried its modern meaning at that time.
9. Ibid., ll. 439–41.
10. Ibid., ll. 469–80. I have disagreed with Elisabeth Brewer's translation of l. 476: 'And now three accusations are made against you.'
11. Ibid., ll. 487–92.
12. Elisabeth Brewer's translation has Gawain shouting, not shrinking. I prefer F. J. Furnivall's reading, 'Thou shontest', meaning 'flinchest' (l. 460).
13. That tail-rhyme romances are not courtly is apparent, for example, in *Libeaus Desconus*, edited by M. Mills, Early English Text Society 261 (1969), and 'Sir Percival of Galles', edited by W. H. French and C. B. Hale in *The Middle English Metrical Romances*, Vol. 2 (New York, 1964). The incomprehension of courtly manners found in tail-rhyme romances is parodied in Chaucer's 'Tale of Sir Thopas' in *The Canterbury Tales*.
14. Elisabeth Brewer's translation gives my reading of ll. 157–62, while F. J. Furnivall assigns to the court the assertion that beheading the knight would be evil. Accepting his punctuation, we have, at the level of fantasy, not a recoil, but the condemnation of the court, including the king. The ambiguous lines, giving Furnivall's punctuation, are as follows:

> "I shall strike his necke in tooe,
> the head away the body froe."
>   thé bade him all be still,
> saith, "Kay, of thy dints make noe rouse,
> thou wottest full litle what thou does;
>   noe good, but Mickle ill."

15. *The Grene Knight*, ll. 214–222. Its being Gawain's danger would make more sense at the imaginative level, but my own interpretation is supported by Elisabeth Brewer's translation. The relevant lines are as follows:

> sore sicke fell Arthur the King,
> and for him made great mourning
>   that into such bale was brought.
>
> the Queen, shee weeped for his sake;
> sorry was Sir Lancelott dulake,
>   & other were dreery in thought
> because he was brought into great perill;
> his mightye manhood will not availe,
>   that before hath freshlye fought.

16. *The Grene Knight*, lines 101–5. The porter says to the king:

> . . . "in lifes dayes old or younge,
>   such a sight I haue not seene!
>
> "for yonder att your gates right;"
> he saith, "hee is a venterous Knight;
>   all his vesture is greene."

17. Ibid., lines 442–4.

> the greene knight rode another way;
> he transposed him in another array,
> before as it was greene.

18. F. J. Furnivall, see note 3 above, p. 77n.
19. The points raised here are of interest also in the study of nineteenth-century children's literature, where fantasies are often transformed by didactic, evangelical purposes. I discuss two such stories, Christoph von Schmid's *The Basket of Flowers* and Elizabeth Wetherell's *The Wide, Wide World*, in *Signal: Approaches to Children's Books*, no. 38, May, 1982.

CHAPTER
[7]

1. See Ernest Jones, *Hamlet and Oedipus* (Gollancz, London, 1949). Jones' approach is one akin to character analysis, but his particular expertise also leads him to note the repetition of character and thought in the play. My own analysis of the structures in the play, and my close textual study support many of the results of Jones. Jones' results are strikingly different from my own in the following instances: he suggests that Hamlet's strategy defeats its own purpose and brings him to destruction; he suggests that Hamlet kills Claudius once the queen is dead and lost to him for ever, and he also suggests that Hamlet's delay is due to his inability to punish the man who has carried out his own murder wish. Since I regard the fundamental structure of the play as magical, the hero arranging events so as to resolve inner conflicts, I see Hamlet as having a strategy which succeeds and a period of delay which is purposeful. Where the queen's death is concerned, the hero acquires the resolution to act immediately after the death of each of the women – accepting Laertes' challenge after Ophelia's death, and killing Claudius after the queen's – so it seems that the deaths of the women, along with that of Claudius, play an important role in his arrangements for a vengeance to be carried out primarily on himself.

   Other interesting, more recent, psychological discussions of *Hamlet* are to be found in Theodore Lidz, *Hamlet's Enemy: Madness and Myth in 'Hamlet'* (Vision Press, London, 1975), a psychiatrist's full study of the theme of madness in the play; and Ari Erlich, *Hamlet's Absent Father* (Princeton University Press, 1977), which challenges Freud's and Jones' Oedipal interpretations, seeing *Hamlet* as dealing with a complex, partially unconscious search for a strong father, rather than with repressed parricidal impulses.

   Freud's own work on *Hamlet* is to be found in 'The Interpretation of Dreams' (1900), in *The Standard Edition of the Complete Psychological Works of Sigmund Freud*, ed. J. Strachey (London, 1953), Vol. V, pp. 60, 175, 263n., 264–6, 444.
2. *Hamlet*, in the edition of Shakespeare's complete works by Charles Jasper Sisson (Odham's Press, 1953), IV, 5, 108.
3. Ibid., V, 2, 233–5.
4. Ibid., II, 2, 62–5.
5. Ibid., IV, 5, 23–39.
6. Ibid., III, 2, 108–9.
7. Ibid., V, 2, 65 and III, 2, 355.
8. Similarly, the heroine of *The Goose-Girl* does not use the punishment of the waiting-maid for her solution; her acknowledged self undergoes the ritual involving punishment.
9. *Hamlet*, III, 2, 411–12.
10. Ibid., V, 1, 1–238.

11. Geoffrey Bullough (ed.), *Narrative and Dramatic Sources of Shakespeare* (London, 1973), Vol. 7, Introduction, pp. 3ff.
12. For the version of Saxo Grammaticus, see Geoffrey Bullough, as in note 11 above, pp. 60ff.; see also Sir Israel Gollancz (ed.), *The Sources of Hamlet* (London, 1926), pp. 94ff., in Latin and in translation. See also Oliver Elton (trans.), *The First Nine Books of the Danish History of Saxo Grammaticus* (London, 1894), pp. 104–30.
13. For Belleforest's version, see Sir Israel Gollancz, as in note 12 above, pp. 166ff. The English version of this work, *The Hystorie of Hamblet*, dated 1608, is included, and it is also to be found in Geoffrey Bullough, see note 11 above, pp. 81ff.
14. See Geoffrey Bullough, as in note 11 above, pp. 15–16.
15. Thomas Kyd, *The Spanish Tragedy*, ed. J. R. Mulryne (New Mermaids, 1970).
16. See Geoffrey Bullough, as in note 11 above, pp. 80–1, for a translation of the relevant passage.
17. *An Icelandic-English Dictionary* (Oxford, 1957) has: 'Amlóði, (1) the true name of the mythological prince of Denmark; (2) Now used metaph. of an imbecile, weak person.' In Norwegian, 'amlod' means: jester, fool; one who often causes harm or mischief, or who afflicts or torments people (*Norsk Ordbok*, Det Norske Samlaget, Oslo, 1966).
18. Sir Thomas Hoby, *The Book of the Courtier*, by Count Baldassare Castiglione (1561), in Everyman's Library, no. 807. There is also a translation by George Bull (Penguin Books, 1967).
19. Grimaldus Goslicius, *The Counsellor*; the copy of this book in the Huntington Library is accessible on University Microfilm no. 14323, Case 41, Roll 244.
20. For a discussion of these contemporary affairs, see Geoffrey Bullough, as in note 11 above, pp. 40–5.
21. See Belleforest's version, Sir Israel Gollancz, as in note 12 above, p. 266.
22. *Hamlet*, V, 2, 64–5. The election system is also referred to in V, 2, 366–7.
23. See Sir Israel Gollancz, as in note 12 above, p. 200.
24. See Geoffrey Bullough, as in note 11 above, pp. 51–2.
25. Albert B. Weiner (ed.), *William Shakespeare, 'Hamlet', The First Quarto, 1603* (New York, 1962), pp. 138–9; 148–9.
26. Dr Theodore Lidz gives similar attention to 'the second part' of the Amleth story in his study *Hamlet's Enemy: Madness and Myth in 'Hamlet'* (see note 1), pp. 140–1. He sees similarities and differences between the dilemmas of the princess of Britain and Ophelia, and also a relationship between Hermutruda and the Player Queen.
27. The name 'Feng' is suggestive of the Norse word 'Fá, fekk (pl. fengu), pret. subj.: fengja (mod. fengi)' = To get, procure, fetch, catch.
28. There is evidence that the ghost may have appeared in the earlier play of *Hamlet*. See Geoffrey Bullough, as in note 11 above, p. 24. In 1596 Thomas Lodge, in his *Wits Miserie*, writes: 'as pale as the Visard of the ghost which cried so miserably at the Theatre like an oister-wife, Hamlet, revenge.'
29. Jan Kott, in his essay ' "Hamlet" of the Mid-century' in *Shakespeare Our Contemporary* (Methuen, and also Doubleday, 1964; University Paperback, 1967) has a fine discussion on how much meaning the play may carry.

TOWARDS A CONCLUSION

1. In *Signal: Approaches to Children's Books*, no. 36 (September, 1981) and no. 38 (May, 1982).
2. E. E. Evans-Pritchard, *Witchcraft, Oracles and Magic Among the Azande* (Oxford University Press, 1937).
3. Keith Thomas, in his *Religion and the Decline of Magic* (Weidenfeld and Nicholson, London, 1971, and Peregrine Books, 1978), Chapter 22, points out that many systems of thought, 'and not only primitive ones', have a 'self-confirming

character', once their initial premises are accepted, they possess a resilience which makes them immune to external argument.
4. There is also a reluctance to acknowledge that we are anything but rational, a reluctance arising from fear of our irrationality. This can set up defences such as denial and repression, and also rationalization, frequently used as a defence. Another reason why fantasy is ignored might be that it is simply unconscious. I have preferred to think in terms of 'unawareness', which has more practical use for my study, but the limited scope of fiction has given me little firm information about either condition.
5. I discuss *Jack and the Beanstalk* in my article in *Signal: Approaches to Children's Books*, no. 36, September, 1981.

INDEX

Alteration in magical storytelling, 31, 94, 98–107; elaboration, 30, 102–3; simplification, 103–4; syncope, 135–9
Amleth, stories of, 126–35, 135–9 passim
Beauty and the Beast, 38, 41, 46, 65
Brer Rabbit tales, 25
Disguise, 26, 33, 38, 86, 87, 102, 120, 121, 131, 136, 137, 141, 143
Emperor's New Clothes, The, 15, 21–2, 23
Exile, 37, 48, 50, 57, 58, 63–4
Exorcism, 44, 49, 58–60, 84, 86–7, 148
Freud and other psychoanalysts, 7, 11, 24–5, 26, 67, 114, 147–8, 152
Gawain and the Green Knight, Sir, 35, 65, 93, 81, 93–113, 140
Golden Bird, The, 49
Goose-Girl, The, 10–11, 17–33, 37–8, 40, 42, 47, 49, 54, 140, 152
Grene Knight, The, 35, 94, 98–107
Hamlet, 11–12, 13, 33, 35, 113, 114–126, 129, 130, 132–3, 135–9, 142
Hero, heroine of magical fantasy, 10, 15–16, 28, 40–1, 103, 105, 118, 142; acknowledged, 32, 38, 49, 118–19, 134, 136, 152; unacknowledged, 32, 38, 48, 49, 56, 118–19, 134, 136
Hobbit, The, 71
Identification in magical fantasy (as the key to the viewpoint), 10, 13, 15–16, 28, 88, 103, 105, 118
Imagery of magical fantasy, 15, 16, 32, 37, 38, 42–3, 45, 46, 54–5, 55–6, 63, 64–5, 97–8, 102, 103, 104, 131, 133, 135
Imagination, 7–8, 16. See also: Intellectual thought in story
Intellectual thought in story, definitions of the imagination, 7–9, 16, 34; as creating the story, 21–2, 23, 25–6, 27, 40, 62–3, 65–6, 70–1, 79–80, 91; transforming fantasy material, 52–3, 60, 89–93, 104–6, 111–13, 121–4, 139, 142–3; discrepancy of intention, 43–4, 62, 66–8, 106. See also: Rationalization, as part of the story
Jack and the Beanstalk, 142
Jane Eyre, 12, 33–4, 47, 48–61, 113
King Horn, 48–9, 57–8
King of the Golden Mountain, The, 38
King Solomon's Mines, 46
Loathly Lady stories, 38, 46, 65, 82–7, 93
Lord of the Rings, The, 34–5, 69, 70–81, 94, 107–10, 111–13 passim
Magic, the characteristics of magical thought (fantasy), 10–11, 15–16, 28, 38, 40–1, 60, 62–3, 64–5, 141; magical object (talisman), 11, 15, 32, 38, 142; magic words, 11, 15, 32, 38, 59, 87, 105, 142. See also: Exorcism, Ritual and Transformation scene
Magical story (fantasy), definitions, 7–12, 15–16, 71, 108–9, 121, 142, 152; characteristics, 22, 26, 28, 32–3, 41–3, 60, 84, 87, 93, 105, 106–7, 118; magical story structures, 31–3, 37–8, 46, 48–9, 96–7
Marriage of Sir Gawaine, The, 82, 85–6
Moves, 31–2, 37, 40, 48–51, 51–60 passim, 63–4, 96–7, 102, 134–5, 142
Names in magical fantasy, 50, 53, 79, 125, 133, 134, 138

Place of adventure, 37, 42, 48–9, 50, 54, 96
Rationalization, as part of the story, 37–8, 40, 42, 43–4, 56–7, 84, 106, 111, 131–2, 142; on the part of critics and audiences, 24, 25, 84, 140–1, 143
Rebecca, 148
Recognition in magical fantasy, 31, 64–5, 87, 97–8, 103
Ritual in magical fantasy, 23–4, 26–33 passim, 37, 38, 44, 45, 46–7, 49, 60, 84, 87, 103, 107, 142, 143

Shadow, The, 34, 60–1, 62, 66–9
She, 34, 37–47, 142
Splitting, 33, 38, 43, 53–4, 118–19, 134
Tale of Florent, 82, 85–6
Transformation scene (shapeshift), 38, 40, 41, 44, 46–7, 64–5, 84, 86–7, 97–8, 103
Treasure Island, 27, 40, 79, 118
Ugly Duckling, The, 34, 60, 62–6, 142
Weddynge of Sir Gawen and Dame Ragnell, The, 38, 46, 65, 82, 84–8
Wife of Bath's Tale, The, 11, 34–5, 81, 82–93, 94, 113, 114, 118